THE
ENERGY
BALLOON

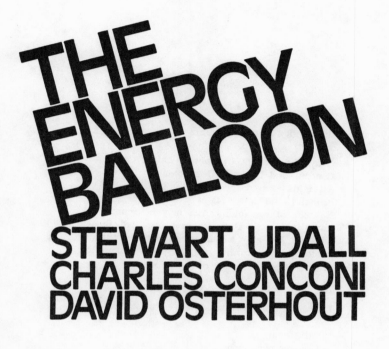

THE ENERGY BALLOON

STEWART UDALL
CHARLES CONCONI
DAVID OSTERHOUT

McGraw-Hill Book Company

New York   St. Louis   San Francisco   Düsseldorf
London   Mexico   Sydney   Toronto

Book design by Marcy J. Katz

123456799BPBP7987654

Library of Congress Cataloging in Publication Data

Udall, Stewart L
   The energy balloon.

    1. Energy policy—United States. 2. United
States—Civilization—1945- 3. Technology and
civilization. I. Conconi, Charles N., joint author.
II. Osterhout, David E., joint author. III. Title.
HD9502.U52U4   333.7′0973   74-14903
ISBN 0-07-065732-7

CONTENTS

59555

FOREWORD

The energy crisis is now part of the common vocabulary of every newspaper reader and television viewer. But the concept first became vivid in my mind in July 1971, when the National Petroleum Council (NPC) issued an alarming report on the U.S. energy future, and Interior Secretary Rogers C. B. Morton commented on the prospect of "a frightening energy scarcity" in the 1980s. During my tenure as Secretary of the Interior, I served for eight years as co-chairman of the NPC (a government-industry study group which included most of the top oil executives), and remembering the uniformly expansive oil outlook of the Council—and of Interior's house experts in the 1960s as well—I was taken aback by the drastic tenor of this report.

In an effort to find out what had happened, I had a long session with Dr. M. King Hubbert, a senior geologist and geophysicist in the United States Geological Survey. Because of the foresight of his predictions on the subject of oil supplies, Dr. Hubbert was being widely quoted by environmentalists. For fifteen years he had been warning that we were grossly overestimating our petroleum resources. Long belittled as a lone pessimist in an industry populated by rabid optimists, Hubbert explained to me that the NPC study had simply publicized the alarming trends he had been predicting all along.

In particular, two major developments were altering the U.S. energy outlook. For one thing, America's production of crude oil had reached an apparent peak in November 1970, and for the first time in their history the oilmen were confronting limits to the further growth of their industry. The second trend was global, but it was beginning to have an impact on the U.S. situation. As an outgrowth of the huge increases in oil consumption by the other industrialized countries, the world marketplace had been converted into a seller's market: the organization of Oil Producing and Exporting Countries (OPEC) had acquired the economic muscle and aggressiveness it needed to demand higher prices and to develop specific plans to acquire part or all of the concession rights of the international oil companies.

The more I studied the problem, the more it was plain that nearly all of the government-industry energy assumptions of the 1960s were wildly optimistic. I had been assured again and again by Interior's experts that there was plenty of domestic oil to take care of our needs at least until the year 2000, and my conversations with the heads of the big international oil companies conveyed the unwavering assurance that "their" reserves abroad were so vast there was nothing to worry about even in the long run.

As I reflected on Hubbert's prescient predictions and evaluated his estimate that the oil-rich U.S. had already used up nearly half of the domestic petroleum that would ever be discovered, I was staggered by the magnitude of this development. My own analysis confirmed Hubbert's thesis, and I became increasingly critical of the support I had mistakenly lent to the boomer psychology of the oilmen. OPEC had always been ridiculed by my advisors—and I had done nothing to counteract their shortsightedness. Having thus helped lull the American people into a dangerous overconfidence, I felt a moral duty to admit my own errors and to expose the wildly optimistic assumptions that had misled the country. It was clear to me that an enormous energy balloon of inflated promises and boundless optimism had long since lost touch with any mainland reality. The widening gap between diminishing resources and a runaway waste economy had reached frightening proportions. There could no longer be any doubt that a vast miscalculation was carrying the country to the brink of crippling shortages—shortages which might have been avoided by a realistic evaluation of our actual resources.

These convictions caused me to begin writing and lecturing about the energy problem in the fall of 1971. The months went by and I became increasingly outspoken. As the bargaining power of the oil exporting countries grew before my eyes, as U.S. oil production continued to decline, and as I grasped for the first time that cheap petroleum had made the whole postwar "miracle of technology" possible, the energy impasse loomed even larger. It would, I was convinced, change the entire pattern of American life.

One current contention of the boomers, however, made me pause. When the oil outlook dimmed, the professional mythmakers developed a new fallback scenario of superabundance. Using paper projections, they pointed out that the U.S. owned one-third of the world's coal reserves and vast deposits of shale which could be processed into enormous quantities of natural gas and trillions of barrels of oil. With an assist from American technology, they claimed, these "alternate sources" of energy would replace petroleum and postpone any threat of shortages until at least "late in the twenty-first century."

This was the kind of soothing advice the American people wanted to hear in the winter of 1974, and "alternate sources" became a popular quick-fix phrase of the energy experts. The economist, always the confident leaders of the growth brigade, quickly calculated that once U.S. crude oil was priced above $8 a barrel, "alternate sources" would be tapped and would swell the energy stream. This, I knew, was another illusion that could mislead the country. I had supervised most of the federal coal programs (including the research effort to develop coal gasification and liquefication) and had wrestled for eight years with the obstacles to the exploitation of oil shale. I thus had first hand knowledge of the problems and pitfalls facing these two troubled industries. It seemed clear that economic and ecological limitations would preclude coal or oil shale from ever becoming meaningful substitutes for petroleum. Petroleum is a nonpariel resource: it is pumped, not mined; and it is found in huge natural fields, not narrow seams covered by tons of earth. Simple logic forced me to the conclusion that this century would see no real substitutes for petroleum on this planet.

In early 1974 these judgments prompted me to plan a forceful statement that would lay the real facts about the energy crisis before the American people and point the way toward possible solutions. The subject was complex, however, and smothered in technicalities, and I realized that if an outspoken book were to be researched and written, I lacked the time to do the job entirely by myself.

Happily, my debates and discussions had brought two incisive young men into my circle. One, Charles Conconi, is a journalist and lecturer; the other, David Osterhout, is a writer and legislative specialist. Both had worked on Capitol Hill and knew the congressional scene, and each of them had the kind of insights which complemented mine and the kind of environmental awareness which made us natural collaborators.

Together we argued and thrashed our way through the welter of current information—much of it confused, misdirected, or misinformed—and finally emerged with what we hope is a committed and opinionated book. It has been written both as a provocative position paper and a detailed outline of imperative reforms and changes. Our purpose in deflating the energy balloon has not been to please, but to challenge vested interests; not to confirm, but to question assumptions; not to entertain, but, hopefully to illuminate the issues.

Stewart L. Udall

INTRODUCTION

When a democracy is floundering, the best way to confront and resolve great issues is through a contest of advocates and a search for the facts. What we are calling the energy crisis may very well be the most complex issue the nation has had to face in this century—a complexity reflected in the cross-currents and confusing counsels at the highest levels of government and industry. This book has been written in the belief that the one sure way to bring the major issues and decisions into focus is for those who perceive problems differently and advocate different solutions to stake out their positions with candor and express their judgments forcefully.

It is very difficult to comprehend all the interrelated facts and issues which are part of the energy problem. The subject is vast, and to discuss it intelligently one must have a grasp of the intricacies of the international oil industry; an understanding of the intertwined energy threads which run through our transportation system, our industrial system, and the energy-dependent lifestyles we have developed in this country; and an acquaintance with such seemingly trivial facts as the comparative amounts of energy consumed by an electric shave and a manual, hot-water shave.

Many first-rate books and articles have been written in recent years about various facets of the energy problem. A perceptive book on nuclear power or an insightful article on the state of the art of coal gasification, however, does not provide the perspective one needs to make judgments on the larger issues, just as an excellent analysis of any important technical problem does little to help citizens evaluate our long-range needs.

Penetrating insights into the oil industry are also indispensable if one desires to come to grips with the big issues. Over three-fourths of our energy in 1974 came from oil and natural gas and the crisis itself centers on this vulnerable industry. Belatedly, the American people have recognized that this is the richest, most powerful, most secretive industry in this country. It touches the lives of almost everyone, it is crucial to the success of our economy, and it is more "affected with a public interest" than any other industry—yet it is not regulated in the public interest.

The petroleum industry also has a self-generated mystique which gives us a misleading impression of its prowess: its new oil fields are invariably referred to as "vast"; potential U.S. petroleum resources are always described as "fabulous" or "boundless"; and it is usually hinted that the largest "strikes" are yet to be made. The machismo of the oil industry is faltering these days, but its youthful feats and inimitable braggadocio are now more a part of the problem than part of the solution to the problem.

We have written this book with a strong point of view, based on conservative assumptions we believe must now shape our policies. We have deliberately expressed outspoken judgments on the major issues, alternatives and controversies. We fully realize these judgments will be tested in the daily events and developments of the months ahead. Events may prove us wrong on some issues and right on others. We have a paramount conviction, however, that taking a polar position will ignite creative disputes and force the professional optimists to defend their positions. This book will have served its purpose if it becomes an anvil on which rational policies for the future can be hammered out.

An argumentative book is urgent because the energy problem is permeated with doubt. The evidence is piling up that the plunder of U.S. petroleum is a great historical blunder. The nation has been looting this prime resource with wanton abandon, and the Arab oil embargo warned us that our voracious consumption cannot continue. Yet even now there are many experts who dispute this contention and who pretend that the big petroleum joyride is still in its early stages.

Confusion has dominated public discussion of the energy problem because experts grinding special axes have offered divergent solutions for the crisis. The oil and coal industries, for example, blame governmental policies and the environmentalists for the shortages and avow they can play a game of energy "catch-up" if they are given additional economic incentives. Most congressmen, on the other hand, appear to agree with consumer advocate Ralph Nader that "the world is drowning in oil" and that the greedy oil companies are perpetrating a "hoax" on the American people.

When one considers our recent history such bewilderment is understandable. The U.S. has taken cheap energy completely for granted for three decades now: cheap gasoline, cheap natural gas, and cheap electric power seemed to be the birthright of every American. There was also the conviction (nurtured to maturity by the space race) that scientists and engineers had arranged for power to be at our fingertips. This belief has its roots deep in the American mind. Once we had the big technology know-how (and had stated openly we would share it with others in due course), there seemed to be nothing unreasonable about the idea that the small fraction of humanity living in the United States of America should own half the automobiles in the world, use over 50 percent of its gasoline, participate in half of its air travel, own half of its television sets and air conditioners, and aspire to double the total energy used every fourteen or fifteen years.

In short, Americans developed a technological hubris which supported the unswerving belief we could literally "do whatever we wanted to do." Not surprisingly, this soaring faith in science persuaded the American people in the winter of 1974 to believe the energy shortage was due to some short-term miscalculation, or was perhaps the result of overreaching by the big oil companies. How, these skeptical citizens asked, could the world's number one oil nation—a country that had just seen its automobile industry set a new record for production—lack the fuel it needed for its basic mode of transportation? How, indeed, could the nation that had developed sophisticated machines to put men on the moon find itself with empty gas pumps and push-buttons that did not produce instant power? These were reasonable questions. The American experience of the past thirty years had been one of building bigger things, of achieving fresh technological "miracles," and of living in a world of abundance.

Given such arrogance, it was foreseeable that our leaders would delude themselves about the energy issue. Such self-deception made it easy to attempt to make an oil policy without deciding how much petroleum the country had left. It also enabled the President to command the oil industry to schedule big increases in production in the 1970s without knowing whether it was either possible or in the national interest for it to do so. Finally, self-deception made it possible for some economists and energy experts to reassure their fellow citizens that alternative energy sources could be cranked up to replace petroleum without really evaluating the enormous technical, economic and environmental obstacles to such accomplishments.

To make matters worse, the great U.S. juggernaut

ploughed ahead as though nothing had changed. Everyone paid lip service to conservation, but nearly everyone continued to operate as though the growth-assumptions of the past were sacrosanct: the doubling of the U.S. demand for petroleum by 1985 was treated as undisputable fact; the plans of the auto-makers for a doubling of the number of cars in this country well before the year 2000 were regarded as sacred writ; and the plans of the petrochemical, air transport and other industries for a doubling and later redoubling of their products and services were regarded as certainties for which the energy industries had to prepare.

"Grow-or-die" has been the unspoken energy slogan. The near insanity of the future scenario envisioned by the big oil companies is indicated by the fact that at the moment the Yom Kippur Arab-Israeli war broke out in October 1973, their "game plan" to meet the incredibly growing oil needs of the nation was reliance on imports of "cheap Arab oil."

In our opinion, there are hoaxes which surround the U.S. energy crisis. However, most of them are larger and more reckless than the manipulations of the oil companies. There is the hoax that we can continue to consume a third of the world's petro-leum by big increases in domestic output. There is the hoax that the scandalous waste which permeates our whole energy system cannot be eliminated with-out damaging our "standard of living." And there is the hoax of some economists and the oilmen who argue that a meaningful national energy policy can be hammered out by the operation of supply and demand in the marketplace without crushing the consuming public or relying on energy conservation measures.

Once the hoaxes and outdated assumptions are pierced and the true alternatives are defined, the people will make the right choices. When this occurs, they will perceive that the era of abundance is over and that the nation must relearn the practice of energy conservation. They will also realize that the U.S. has been wrong to base energy plans on "cheap" imported oil, on "vast" undiscovered oil fields, and on the inflated extrapolations of anonymous petroleum geologists. They will perceive, as well, that it is an act of improvidence to base our energy policy in the next decade on Arab oil, or gasified coal, or oil processed from oil shale.

We have attempted in this book to develop a positive program for a lean America. We are aware that the implementation of transitional changes of this magnitude presents an unprecedented peacetime challenge. We are confident, however, that there will be an invigorating response once the true alternatives and options are presented to the American people.

CHARLES N. CONCONI
DAVID E. OSTERHOUT
STEWART L. UDALL
Washington, D.C.
June 1974

chapter one

THE AMERICAN PAGEANT
OF WASTE

". . . One of the freedoms that we have in this country is the freedom of mobility. I can name the other four freedoms, but certainly the freedom to move as one chooses is one of the freedoms that we enjoy in this country. I still believe there will be a Cadillac. I still believe the Cadillac will be a standard to the world. I still think that a 12-year-old boy in this great country of ours will be reaching for the top. . . ."

—Mack Worden
General Motors Marketing Vice President

"It seems to me we've been living in a fool's paradise. I think the day of super-affluence, and super-consumption, is gone."

—Rev. Theodore M. Hesburgh
April 1974

Because we are a society that revels in the superlative, the exceptional, the grandiose, the most representative relics of our time will not be found in the display cases of the Smithsonian Institution in Washington, D.C., storehouse of the artifacts of American history. Rather they will be seen in the ravaged landscape and in the vainglorious structures and machines we have left behind.

Future generations will undoubtedly marvel at our extravagance—ever taller buildings, ever longer and heavier automobiles, ever bigger and faster airplanes —like some Ozymandias of the twentieth century. It was all part of our cherished belief that the most powerful and successful nation in history deserved to have the biggest and best of everything. To fuel the giddy, go-go philosophy of superconsumption, huge quantities of imported and domestically produced energy and raw materials were used with such a wanton disregard for conservation and efficiency that the United States became the wastrel nation of the world.

Historians will look back on 1973 as the year the era of cheap energy ended and Americans began to confront the illusion that unlimited energy would always be available. It was also the year we realized that cheap, abundant energy was the all-pervasive factor in making the United States' success story the adventure of the ages. For the United States, it would mark a turning point—a new maturation and awareness of a bitter truth: we had overshot and were making an overdraft on our own, and the world's, resources.

Living in the most affluent soceity in history, Americans took large amounts of the resources of the globe and became the best clothed, housed, fed, transported, and entertained people in the world.

It was, however, never enough. The American people were insatiable. They demanded more of everything: taller buildings; extravagant space programs; more powerful, luxurious autos; weed-free lawns; second houses; boats—everything. And this spiral still didn't bring contentment.

In postwar America, technology was holy writ. No problem was so complex that it couldn't be solved through more ingenious technology: though today's technology was wonderful, tomorrow's would hold even better surprises. From the White House on down, technological optimism permeated our society and shaped the aims of the country. The last four Presidents were at the center of things in Washington during the 1950s, when such optimism was at its peak. It was no wonder, then, that President Eisenhower considered the construction of the massive interstate highway system as the major domestic achievement of his administration. Presidents Kennedy and Johnson thought the lavishly financed space program was the most significant attainment of their years in office. And when President Nixon genuflected before U.S. technology and greeted the Apollo XII astronauts who had walked on the moon with the classic hyperbole, "This is the greatest week since the creation of the earth!" technology had its ultimate enthronement. The cost in energy and resources of this exhibitionist adventure was absurdly wasteful. Perhaps one day the space race will be looked on as the last hurrah of a technically intoxicated society and one of the great publicity stunts of the ages.

If the space race expressed the ideology that we had the wealth and cheap energy and technical skill to accomplish any goal, the cult of the automobile symbolized our faith in an economic system based on the maximum production and consumption of goods. That, presumably, was what our economic system was all about.

It was the halcyon period of U.S. affluence—U.S. citizens congratulated themselves daily that they were a nation on wheels, the most mobile people in the history of the world. The U.S. had half the automobiles in the world, and used over 50 percent of the gasoline. The U.S. had more than half the commercial jet aircraft, and Americans participated in more than half the air travel.

In the dazzling quest for the biggest and fastest, the U.S. Senate's decision in 1971 to say no to the Supersonic Transport was a beginning of wisdom. Although the SST was defeated in a bitterly fought debate, ironically it was defeated because of potential environmental and economic risks. The energy crisis was not yet apparent, and little argument was made about the fuel required for high speed travel, even though it was the champion gas-guzzler of all times.

During the 1950s and 1960s, energy and growth discussions focused on the seemingly limitless expansion possibilities. It was generally reasoned that with American know-how nearly anything was possible. Few leading scientific, economic or social figures felt the need to worry about supplies of petroleum because of impressive new oil finds in the Middle East and in other parts of the world. It was further reasoned, with bemused indulgence, that atomic energy "Atoms for Peace" would eventually provide an "inexhaustible" source of clean, cheap energy. Such optimism encouraged the adoption of a lifestyle comfortably indifferent to consumption and waste. Then we flaunted and exported the American formula for success as the "how to do it" example for the world.

When an occasional Jeremiah accused affluent Americans of wanton greed, the ingenious, convincing rationale of the conventional economists was that the way to uplift our poor—and ultimately the standard of living of the poor countries as well—was to produce more. It was reasoned that greater production would create a bigger economic pie and result in wider distribution of goods. And no one would have to sacrifice current satisfactions. It was a "we can have our cake and gorge on yours too" philosophy because we would magnanimously share the wonders of American technology and soon the world would enjoy the benefits of U.S.-style progress.

But technology demands energy, and in the harsh projection statistics of the period, multiplying patterns of consumption are so great that in the 1970s alone the world will burn up as much oil as was used in the hundred years from 1870 to 1970. At the present rate of consumption, these demands are expected to double in the 1980s, but it is not possible for supplies to keep up with such increasing pressures.

Until the Arab oil embargo, most Americans were convinced the great energy joyride would continue indefinitely. For many Americans the abrupt embargo marked the first warning that cheap, abundant oil, the real secret of the country's postwar success, might run short.

We would do well to document what it was like when we were at the peak of the energy binge because our grandchildren might scoff at reports of two or more cars in many families, of automobile engines with only 20 percent fuel-burning efficiency, with the heaviest models getting as little as seven miles to a gallon of gasoline. They might find it incredible that ornamental natural gas lanterns burned twenty-four hours a day in hundreds of thousands of front yards and that pilot lights on kitchen stoves consumed up to one-third of the gas used annually in the average gas range. Or that we allowed and even encouraged the construction of sealed glass skyscrapers that required around-the-clock environmental "climate control"—buildings which surpassed the energy demands of cities as large as 150,000 in population. Who will be able to explain the vast megastructures—sports palaces, super jetports, and enclosed shopping centers —designed by buoyant architects and builders who believed there would always be cheap energy to make their creations comfortable year-round? How will we describe the dogma of unlimited growth, based on the tenet of an ever-expanding Gross National Product that rapturously breeched the trillion-dollar mark? What was a "standard of living," and who established that ours was the correct one? How will we ever rationalize the thousands of pounds of fertilizer dumped on suburban lawns and golf courses while starving nations had meager yields from exhausted crop lands desperately in need of fertilization?

It was all part of the age of U.S. affluence, when most Americans assumed the national interest was served by finding ways to spend more, to consume more, to reach for an easier life with more comfort, recreation and gadgetry. It was computed that U.S. energy consumption was so vast that it was tantamount to every citizen having 200 personal servants attending him.

It was not surprising that one of the major dilemmas that attracted considerable attention during the golden 1960s was how Americans were going to deal with all the leisure time that energy-draining computers and sophisticated machines were going to give them. The four-day work week and the marvelous machines which did virtually all the physical work would alter the national lifestyle for the remaining decades of the century. The success formula was fixed —if any technical problems appeared, omniscient American technologists would solve them.

The spiraling American dream was not just a back-and-forth-to-work car for Dad, but a supermarket and haul-the-kids station wagon for Mom. Many older teenagers had their own cars, and some high schools developed traffic congestion and parking problems to rival those of city business districts. For those too young to drive, there were new trail motorbikes or off-the-road motorcycles, promoted through slick advertising as a good way for fathers and sons to "get back to nature" doing the kind of things fathers and sons should do. But the mood was set and a people intoxicated with motion bought trail bikes, snowmobiles, and dune buggies by the millions.

Much of the script for the golden age of American affluence was written by copywriters in advertising firms. Advertising created demand, and corporate America responded with products manufactured to self-deteriorate so the sales chart could keep climbing. The emphasis, of course, was on convenience, comfort and superficiality of styling change.

This uniquely American concept of planned obsolescence changed our values and created a throwaway society. It made junky "new" models of everything seem desirable, it put a premium on the fast turnover of goods, and it debunked—practically debunked as un-American—the thrifty idea of product durability. A new U.S. institution was born, and the "new improved" everything whipped manufacturing to new heights.

In the affluent American society there was a motorized gadget to do nearly everything. There was power to mow the lawn and make the coffee, open the cans, mix the drink, polish the shoes, brush the teeth and comb the hair. Not only did the United States have more television sets, refrigerators and other appliances than all the rest of the world's people put together, the country was so rich that nearly everyone had them.

According to the 1970 census, 99.8 percent of all American families owned a refrigerator, 95 percent at least one television set (while 37.8 percent owned a colored one) and 80 percent at least one car. Between 1960 and 1970, Americans bought 47 million hair-dryers; we had half the television sets in the world and were generating and using 40 percent of the world's electricity.

In the late '60s and early '70s, even the ecology movement—with its call for Americans to seek harmony with nature—became a victim of the wasteful consumption pattern. Thousands of Americans bought thundering snowmobiles and powerboats and motorcycles, hooked them to the rear of lumbering all-the-comforts-of-home Winnebagos, and headed for the country, where they clustered in paved camp sites in the instant "Walden Pond" industry that fed this new interest.

The consumption of electricity is a key index to the rate at which the nation uses energy. In the period 1946 to 1968, the consumption of electricity per person rose some 436 percent, while the national population increase for the same period was 43 percent and the Gross National Product was 59 percent. Since the demand growth rate greatly exceeds the population or business growth and production rates, the simple conclusion is that an increasingly higher standard of living is demanding more electric energy—a demand that is doubling every six or seven years, while the population doubles every seventy years.

What is true for electricity consumption in varying degrees holds true for all other energy sources. The United States is the world's undisputed champion user, waster, producer and consumer of nearly all forms of energy. Although space heating is one of the largest users of energy, between 1960 and 1968 the greatest growth in electrical energy demands came from air conditioners, clothes dryers and the deluge of electrical gadgets.

The United States' growth rate since the end of World War II dramatizes the nation's consumption values and priorities. According to the computations of ecologist Barry Commoner, the highest postwar growth rate is in the production of nonreturnable soda bottles, an increase of 53,000 percent. Production of synthetic fibers came in second with a 5,980 percent increase. Air condition compression units showed a 2,850 percent increase and electric household gadgets were up 1,040 percent.

All these changes in lifestyle and consumption demands from the prewar period to the postwar period represent significant energy demands, especially in the explosive growth of synthetic fibers and in materials like aluminum and cement. It was, for example, a simple manufacturing process to produce cotton cloth. Nylon, on the other hand, requires six to ten chemical reactions operating at temperatures from 200 to 700 degrees Fahrenheit, all demanding large amounts of fuel. Energy-intensive industries are those which use huge amounts of energy for each unit of production. Such industries—primary metals like steel and aluminum, chemicals, paper, cement, the petroleum industry, food processing and packaging—account for 80 percent of industrial energy consumption. Most of the energy goes for process steam, which is not recycled, direct heat or electricity to drive motors—some 90 percent—and in other highly inefficient techniques.

Even in farming and food processing, where success had been so spectacular that mountains of food were stockpiled and many farmers were paid not to produce at all, the energy waste was profound. In the 1970s when ever-growing millions of people are starving, we feed most of our cereal grains to animals to produce meat. Harvard nutritionist Jean Mayer estimates that the same amount of food now feeding 210 million Americans would feed 1.5 billion Chinese on an average Chinese diet.

Each American, for example, now requires 2,200 pounds of grain to feed himself each year, with only 140 pounds of that total eaten directly in cereal products or as grain in bread. The Chinese feeds himself on 400 pounds of grain and eats 360 of it directly as grain. The comparison is not made to argue for the average Chinese diet, but to show that, with nearly half the world going to bed hungry each night, American high-on-the-hog food extravagance is certain to draw deserved withering criticism in the years ahead.

The American diet has turned increasingly to meat; a per person average of 119 pounds was consumed in 1973 as compared to 50 pounds in 1950. Since cereal-fed beef is very wasteful to produce, we consume an inordinate amount of the world's grain supplies.

It is the extensive, complicated business of production, processing and distribution—with canned, frozen, and processed, prepackaged foods becoming a

principal part of our diets—that has made food processing the fourth largest energy consumer in the
country.

Gone is that period in American history when the
bulk of the food a family consumed was produced on
local farms and brought in fresh to small markets and
shops—usually within walking distance for most people—in a very neat, energy-efficient system.

Now our food comes from all points in the country
and from around the world. Almost none of it reaches
us truly fresh. It is grown, processed and transported
in an energy-intensive method requiring substantial
power for cultivation, irrigation, fertilization, harvesting, processing, packaging, transportation and distribution. Moreover, it usually comes to large super-
markets that are generally accessible only by automobile.

It is no wonder U.S. farmers now refer to themselves as agribusinessmen. Gasoline and electric motors are demanded at nearly every step of processing:
they provide power for sophisticated farm machinery
and for trucks used in shipping; they run a vast array
of refrigeration devices, from the frost-free refrigerator in the home to the fast-freeze machinery of the
processing plants to all the equipment used in packaging. This extravagant industrialized food system
requires 5 to 10 calories of energy to produce 1 calorie
of food. If every nation had our energy-intensive food
production system—and we have been advertising our
system as "the way to do it"—the world would use 80
percent of its current energy just to produce food.

Post-World War II consumption is nowhere better

exemplified than in the proliferation of excess high-rise construction, the epitome of extravagance made possible when energy is plentiful and cheap.

Buildings are second only to transportation as the largest user of energy in the United States. Perhaps special legislation can be passed to preserve some of the absurd architectural structures of the period as national historical monuments to our technological arrogance.

Future generations of Americans and tourists from other nations will undoubtedly find the twin 110-story towers of New York City's World Trade Center (with 10 million square feet of floor space) and Chicago's Sears Tower, also 110 stories (the world's tallest building at 1,450 feet and the largest private office building as well), interesting studies in engineering grandiosity and vanity. So, too, will they be fascinated by the $700 million Dallas–Fort Worth airport, which covers 28 square miles and was planned to be "the largest in the universe." The Texas-style Taj Mahal used up enough concrete alone to build several pyramids and was touted as the first twenty-first century air facility. Not to be outdone is the gaudy New Orleans Superdome, which may yet become the champion white elephant structure since the pyramid of Cheops.

Whole cities could have the necessary energy to light and heat homes and businesses on the vast amounts demanded to just run elevators, feed the lighting needs and pump the water up 110 stories to fountains and toilets.

Of course, Chicagoans are delighted with their

black tinted-glass Sears Tower. They have come out on top in the heated battle for possession of the tallest building in the world. It is an ugly, jutting finger of black, visible for miles—and it has a power center that could serve a city larger than Rockford, Illinois' second largest city with a population of 144,000. Civic pride can ignore the gargantuan energy appetite necessary to keep Sears Tower functioning—at least until it becomes too much of a luxury.

It was more than civic pride, however, that produced buildings like Sears Tower and the World Trade Center. It was cheap energy. The owners and designers of these monstrosities assumed the power would always be "on"—and always be cheap. This assumption made energy the ignored factor in architecture and in any aspect of national growth equations. Until the 1973 energy pinch, the oil and electric power companies thought their biggest energy problem was the promotion of the use of more energy. Growth was their primary goal until the Arabs demonstrated that cheap, unlimited energy was not a God-given right of all Americans.

The power and utility companies consequently established special rate structures based on the concept that the more energy a consumer used the less he paid. They thus made it unnecessary for a consumer to worry about the energy needed to keep a Sears Tower or a World Trade Center functioning. Since energy was dirt cheap, there was no need to worry that a machine or production process burns up abnormally vast amounts of energy or that the simple, 100-watt electric light bulb uses only 5 percent of the energy going into it, wasting the remainder in lost heat. It made "good business sense" not to bother wasting time or money conserving energy or finding more energy-efficient industrial or building techniques. All buildings in the United States, for example, on the average burn up annually at least 40 percent more fuel than would be necessary if they were designed, insulated and built to be more energy efficient. And that saving doesn't take account of the fact that most buildings are overheated and overcooled.

In a study of public utility rates in Chicago, home consumers—representing the largest category of users, but burning only 20 percent of the national output—paid 23.4 cents per therm for natural gas. Industrial bulk users, on the other hand, paid 7.1 cents per therm while consuming 40 percent of the national output. This typified the national pattern of energy use for all forms of energy—electricity, heating oil or coal.

A further irony in the ever-compounding tragedy of energy errors is that the power plants producing the energy are themselves grossly inefficient. Power plants that burn fossil fuel—coal and oil—waste more than 60 percent of their fuel burning potential, and the avidly supported nuclear power plants, "the energy sources of tomorrow," have an even worse record. About 70 percent of a nuclear power plant's energy efficiency is poured into the air or into lakes and streams as wasted heat. This heat loss is not only wasteful, it destroys the ecology of the waterways.

Our society has gone on a packaging spree that

wantonly exhausts our energy resources—and produces an enormous amount of trash.

We are a generation of dumpers, and, since archeologists and anthropologists carefully excavate the trash heaps of early civilizations to learn what those societies were like, future civilizations would undoubtedly find the refuse heaps of the United States equally revealing. The problem won't be in finding such trash heaps, but in selecting which of the millions to excavate. Among the slightly used products and packaging that are discarded annually in the United States are 8 million automobiles, 100 million rubber tires, 40 million tons of paper, 48 million cans and 26 million bottles. All of it piles up each year into a 400-billion-pound municipal trash heap.

We are such prodigious trash manufacturers that the production of trash may surpass all other achievements. What a paradoxical accomplishment it will seem to future scholars that each day each citizen of the United States discarded five and one-half pounds of trash and looked forward eagerly to a rate of eight pounds per day per person by 1980—and that most of these "wastes" contained enormous amounts of usable energy.

For municipalities running out of land fills and incinerator capacity, solid waste disposal techniques cost nearly $5 billion yearly. Massive amounts of energy are wasted in the manufacture of single-use bottles, cans and cartons, and in the complicated trash collection and disposal problems that affect every city, town and rural area in the country.

It is not unusual when riding through picturesque back country to see abandoned cars, rotting tires, bottles and cans lying at the bottom of an embankment or fouling a mountain stream. Such refuse is an ugly intrusion on the delicate, natural beauty of our nation. It is a unique kind of disposal problem that makes the thousands of pounds of metal in the car of such little economic value that it is easier and cheaper to abandon the car than to sell it for recycling. In 1971, more than 82,000 old automobiles were left on the streets of New York City to be towed away. The 82,000 cars represent an eightfold increase in the problem since 1963. Other cities across the country have similar problems, and thousands of tons of used metal pile up in thousands of ugly automobile graveyards, rusting in the weather, ignored as a source of raw material for recycling.

The most significant measure of the unbelievable waste in energy and resources is that only about 10 percent of the total amount is recycled.

Computing the problem in dollars (which until the energy shortage was the principal way to judge anything) almost 3½ percent of the nation's Gross National Product in 1966 was spent on all aspects of packaging. This amounted to $25 billion of the country's productive wealth. Of that total, $16.2 billion represented the worth of the raw materials used to produce the packaging. Since 90 percent of the packaging produced is not recycled, in 1966 this country threw away, after using only once, about $14.6 billion. The tax-paying public had to pay another $419 million to local governments to collect and dispose of the discarded material.

Unfortunately, no one has yet adequately computed the energy costs present at every stage of the life of a product—from the extraction of the raw material, to the manufacture and production, to the delivery, discard, pickup, transfer and, finally, to the disposal in some man-made, landfill mountain, open dump or municipal incinerator.

Each year, municipal waste contains some 40 million tons of paper and paperboard, representing the annual destruction of 600 million trees. In addition to paper and wood fibers, the nation's trash cans annually hold 10 million tons of iron, 1 million tons of nonferrous metals and 15 million tons of glass—resources estimated to be worth $1 billion.

In throwaway cans, aluminum is rapidly replacing steel—a change that substitutes an energy-intensive process for a more thrifty one. It has also been estimated that the replacement of the returnable bottle system with the throwaway represents a fourfold or fivefold increase in power consumption.

To further calculate the power cost, the production of a ton of steel from ore requires about 2,700 kilowatt hours. Reclaiming a ton of recycled steel in an electric furnace requires only 700 kilowatt hours. The production of aluminum, on the other hand, requires more than 17,000 kilowatt hours.

While the one-time-use-and-throwaway habit of Americans symbolizes one facet of the profligate lifestyle in the affluent society, surely the automobile is its supreme metaphor. To understand the impact of the automobile on our lives is to understand the United States itself—its successes, values, drives, assumptions, beliefs, dreams and failings. The auto has been the great shaper of postwar America, and it has changed everything from our social habits to our attitudes toward cities.

There is no need for a special proclamation making the automobile the supreme expression of American culture. It has achieved that status all by itself. The venerable Smithsonian Institution already has a section devoted to the history of the motorcar, with nostalgic gasoline pumps and different kinds of paving materials. Some day, no doubt, it will also memorialize the car of the 1970s—massive in size and weight, air conditioned and gadget filled, with energy-draining devices and an inefficient internal combustion engine averaging 12 miles per gallon of gasoline.

The American automobile culture is unique; there never has been anything like it.

Mr. Toad, in the ponderous children's classic, "The Wind in the Willows," knew back in 1908 that the motorcar, with its lovely "poop-poop" horn, had changed his life as it would change the lives of Americans and of other people living in industrial nations throughout the world.

"All those wasted years that lie behind me, I never knew, never even dreamt! But now—but now that I know, now that I fully realize! O, what a flowery track lies spread before me henceforth! What dust-clouds shall spring up behind me as I speed on my reckless way. . . ."

Thus Mr. Toad and his countrymen were on their way in the transportation revolution that became the shaping force of an entire nation, its institutions and its values.

Although a few automobiles existed at the turn of the century, it was Henry Ford in 1908, with the mono-color Model-T, who launched the motorcar age. Before Ford introduced mass production techniques and the Model-T, Oldsmobile was producing two thousand cars a year of its chain-driven, tiller-steered, 20-miles-per-hour, 5-horsepower model. But the Model-T was a phenomenal success—15 million were produced and the United States was on rubber wheels racing through the flowery track with dust-clouds springing up behind. While Ford was selling a rather simple, efficient, reliable car, Alfred T. Sloan, Jr., and General Motors introduced the concepts of variety, style and annual change of models. Sloan sold fantasy through advertising and fathered the concept of planned obsolescence. His approach came to dominate the industry and established a pattern that other industries were to emulate.

The United States would never be the same again. The face of the nation had to change to accommodate the automobile. From the earliest days of the nation, a network of roads and turnpikes carried settlers, merchants and travelers to neighboring towns, states and territories. Travel had been slow and precarious, dependent on the horse and inadequate roads, impassable in bad weather with few direction markers or accommodations.

The motorcar gave freedom, speed and mobility never before experienced in history. We could go anywhere we wanted. We would, like twentieth-century pioneers, move easily beyond the historic confines of the city and take advantage of the open countryside, where land was cheaper and the American dream of a single-unit home with a lawn and trees was within the grasp of most people. For the more affluent the automobile meant an easy commute to a second home in the country or a vacation retreat near an unspoiled lake or an undeveloped forest.

Builders and developers could expand into the neighboring countryside to build suburban communities that were easily accessible from the city. All the while America's automobile population exploded, and with it grew an incredible array of related industries to maintain and service the motorcar and the new society of mobile people who spent their lives in or around their cars. So, too, petroleum demands grew bigger and bigger.

We left the cities behind, stripped of economic support, to stumble and die like mastodons before the advancing ice age. We built a new future in the surrounding undeveloped countryside. When the new suburbs became crowded, overbuilt and tacky, the automobile—and cheap gasoline—made it possible to move even further out to the open land over the next horizon. Business, industry and commercial development, like Klondike camp followers, were never far behind and, in fact, often led the way. It seemed that the only limit to the ugly, unplanned suburban sprawl was the distance we were willing to commute. Unfortunately, there seemed to be no limitation; people showed a willingness to commute longer and longer distances behind the wheel of their motorcars. The only real limitation appeared when builders and developers began to run out of cheap land—and when the U.S. cheap energy binge expired as the Arabs trebled the price of oil. Then, for the first time it became clear that cut-rate low-cost gasoline was the thing that made the whole orgy of urban sprawl possible in the first place.

The megapolis expansion of Washington, D.C., was typical of the kind of sprawl that affected every metropolitan area. Washington began its growth before the postwar era. Into the 1930s the nation's capital was a small, quiet town, Southern and genteel. The pace was slow and the city was active only while Congress was in session. During the humid summers, Congress was in recess and the city's population fell significantly. With the exception of the historic old city of Alexandria, Virginia, to the immediate south, Washington was surrounded by a relatively undeveloped area and by a few small Virginia and Maryland towns.

Then came the Franklin D. Roosevelt administration and the explosive growth of the federal bureaucracy to fight the Great Depression. The population influx of the '30s, further expanded by the

massive military bureaucracy that came for the war
and stayed, spilled beyond Washington into metas-
tasizing suburbs. The small, highly livable, self-contained communities that had existed were swallowed
up and became unidentifiable parts of shapeless counties. Occasionally they were broken by garish commercial strips and shopping plazas, and they had
no recognizable downtowns. They were almost totally
dependent on the automobile. The rush to the suburbs left Washington, as it left other cities throughout
the country, financially and socially strained. The
rich, complex, multifaceted civilization the city made
possible was virtually eradicated.

Throughout history, cities have been man's cultural,
intellectual, recreational and social centers. With all
the emphasis on sprawl, there was no investment
money left to improve or maintain inner-city properties. Residential buildings deteriorated to the point
where it seemed the roaches and rats were competing
for living space with the blacks and poor whites who
were trapped there. With expanding slums and
economic deprivation came crime and violence, offering another excuse for the suburbanite to further
abandon the city.

Instead of the city's ethnic, racial, political, economic polyglot, the suburbanite clustered in homo-
genous communities, where each segment was age
categorized, "price tagged" and isolated into new
kinds of middle- and upper-middle-class ghettoes. The
old concept of neighborhood, a wonderous mixture of
age groups, nationalities, and social status, was de-

stroyed. So too was the precious feeling of community that all the jingoistic Junior Jay-Cees or Welcome Wagons could not put back together again. The singular blandness of suburbia provoked anthropologist Margaret Mead to observe that it might be a good idea to haul grandmothers around in a book-mobile type of trailer so suburban children could see what older people look like.

A completely unique drive-in economy developed. In the automobile human beings were conceived, went to school, rode to first dates, received first kisses, were married, had babies and frequently died. In California, the mecca of the automobile culture, some funeral establishments advertised a drive-in plan: a motorist could drive past a display window to pay his last respects to a dead relative or friend without having to leave his car!

The suburban growth pattern was so erratic and multidimensional that it was impossible for any public transportation system to provide adequate service without losing money. The result was further dependence on the automobile, a fact which, unfortunately, neglected to take into consideration people who were unable to drive—the young, the physically disabled and the aged—often making them virtual prisoners in their cul-de-sac homes.

Many mothers found themselves relegated to the role of chauffeur, as they carted school-age children around the shapeless, freeform suburban communities—to school, church, dancing lessons, scouts, Little League, birthday parties, Y.M.C.A. and the myriad other activities with which children become involved.

For those too old, too poor, or physically unable to drive, life in the suburbs resembled imprisonment. There was no grocery store, dry cleaner, bakery, variety store, doctor or dentist down the street or on the corner. Careful zoning kept merchants, with their helpful delivery boys, out of residential neighborhoods. Shopping was relegated to shopping centers or malls or plazas, and few of these were ever within walking distance. Or else their locations—generally at the crossroads of highspeed, multilane highways—made approach on foot a foolhardy venture. As for doctors and dentists, they could generally only be found in highrise medical buildings in some distant commercial area.

It was also disconcerting for many suburbanites to discover that the basic public services they took for granted in cities—police, fire and emergency ambulance—were strained by the attempt to cover vast geographic areas. In a medical emergency, it was not at all comforting to know that the hospital was 15 miles away and that the local emergency ambulance service hadn't been able to keep up with the booming growth rate.

In addition, an efficient public transportation system, either within the suburbs or between the suburbs and the center city, was almost totally lacking. The daily commute to work wasted an enormous amount of energy, with 50 million cars on the road each weekday carrying only one person. The automobile, in making itself supreme, destroyed not only a lifestyle, but also what had been a more integrated, efficient system of railroads, trolleys, buses and even pedestrian traffic.

The railroads had once given shape and direction to the country's growth; most people lived along the railroad rights-of-way or within easy access of railroad stops. In fact, thousands of American cities were once served by railroad lines that provided commuter and short-haul as well as transcontinental services. Even though the train was, and still is, a more energy-efficient form of passenger and freight transportation, its effectiveness and even its ability to survive was severely damaged by automobiles, trucks and airplanes powered by cheap petroleum. Buses and trolleys also found the automobile too formidable to oppose and lingered only as curiosities or economically endangered, heavily subsidized enterprises.

Sadly, the biggest loser was the pedestrian. The most efficient, healthy, versatile and energy-saving method of moving about is walking. City streets, bridges and neighborhoods were traditionally designed to accommodate walkers along broad, shaded, protected promenades. Walking gave a person the opportunity to get a feeling for his community and to know his neighbors, the shopkeepers, the merchants and the children. The automobile, however, spread the commercial areas out, making walking obsolete, while suburban communities with miles of freeform, curving streets further discouraged walking by eliminating the sidewalks. In many suburbs children walking to school or to visit a friend have one of two choices—traveling in the street or across neighboring lawns. Neither choice is satisfactory. In cities a pedestrian walking across a river bridge—and few modern bridges make accommodations for walkers—creates such a curiosity that he becomes a hazard to motorists who slow down to watch him.

Just as the vast highway building program expanded to accommodate the growing number of automobiles, so, too, the drive-in economy developed new ways of serving a population on wheels. Drive-in theaters, motels, groceries, banks and thousands of different fast-food enterprises became social and courting centers for a new generation of youth. In 1973 a successful film entitled *American Grafitti* depicted the teenage way of life in a California town during the early '60s. The movie dramatized the automobile culture that centered around a drive-in restaurant. Most of the teenagers' social activity, status and recreation were closely associated with the cars in which they "cruised."

The film's success was due in part to its detailed documentation of the teenage automobile culture. It was a mark of manhood—a ritualistic passage into adulthood—to acquire a driver's license. With the license came liberation, the means to escape the confines of family and community. Nondriving teenagers were dependent on parents or others of driving age to deliver them to school activities, parties, the movies or the local drive-in hangouts. In the monotonous suburbs, rarely served by any adequate form

of public transportation, the emotional strains were
often severe.

With 48 percent of the world's passenger cars,
which in 1970 consumed nearly 55 percent of the
world's gasoline, America was at the mercy of the
motorcar. Every institution in the country felt its
impact. Cars, for example, accounted for 30 percent
of all consumer debts annually and auto-related matters made up nearly 57 percent of the cases in the
U.S. court system.

To provide the extensive road and highway system
demanded by the massive automobile population, a
highway building industry with formidable political
influence arose. Special obeisance to the automobile
was formalized with the establishment of the National
Highway Trust Fund, a governmental program dedi-
cated to one purpose—the construction of the massive
interstate system. As a result, tens of billions of dollars
were spent laying down a network of roads that went
wherever growth-minded developers and politicians
wanted it to go: motorists sped along wide, limited-
access expressways which ran mile after mile through
the countryside, carefully avoiding cities and towns.

While it became easier to streak from one point
to another, the expressways regimented motorists,
keeping them on a well-defined track just as assuredly
as if they were traveling on rails. But while the
traveler was tied to the ground, it made more sense
to compare his experience to that of the airplane
passenger, who also sped from point to point without
getting a feel of what came between. As the late

Texas author Frank Dobie once described it, "The American people don't travel any more—a real traveler smells and savors his surroundings—he's just transported."

By avoiding the small towns and cities along the way, the speeding motorist missed the color and variety that individual communities offer. Instead, all he saw was the monotonous roadside culture of drive-in America.

When he wanted fuel, he stopped at garish turnpike plazas or at interchanges where towering Exxon, Texaco, Shell or Gulf signs literally beckoned him to pause for the quick fill-up.

If he wanted food, he had no real choice. If he didn't opt for the bland, ever-present Howard Johnson's then he patronized some other national food-serving franchise that either monopolized turnpike plazas with the special blessing of the state governments or proliferated at prime locations along major interstate roadways. The food was uniformly tasteless and expensive, but, of more importance to most travelers, it was conveniently served and quickly eaten.

Sleeping accommodations completed the motorist's isolation. It was a rare driver who drove into a city for the night when the major highway interchanges boasted sprawling motel cities; he could choose among Holiday Inns, Quality Courts or Ramada Inns—they were not only hosts from coast to coast but were uniformly the same coast to coast.

It was thus possible to criss-cross America and see

only the edges of cities and a sliver of countryside glimpsed at high speed. It was also possible to have the disconcerting feeling of never having gone anywhere, since the motels, gas stations and restaurants were everywhere alike.

With the vast investments necessary to construct franchise tourist accommodations along the turnpikes and interchanges, the major food and motel corporations were assured of dominating the industry. Such corporate control may have been at the expense of thousands of independent restaurateurs and motel managers, but it supplied speed and efficiency to traveling motorists. In the end, the automobile culture got what it demanded.

The automobile reigned over the American economy. The industry, directly or indirectly, provided roughly one-fifth of all jobs in the United States. But for all its economic advantages the automobile did more to damage and destroy the environment—and life itself—than any other thing. In dominating the national way of life, it proved to be an anti-human device, killing 55,000 people in 1971 and a total of 1.76 million Americans in the past half century— more than twice the number killed on the battlefield throughout our history. There were other human costs as well: direct injuries from accidents and indirect injuries from lethal chemicals pouring out of tailpipes, the din of rolling tires and roaring engines, and the emotional aggravations of traffic jams and parking dilemmas. The automobile truly was a drain on the individual.

The sad irony of the 1960s was that the United States, dependent on an abundant, cut-rate gasoline supply, was the only country in the world to commit itself totally to the automobile culture—mainly because we were producing and gulping down half of the world's crude oil. During the 1960s, the nation's automobile population doubled; in the early '70s it passed 100 million registrations.

The growth of the automobile culture was not accompanied by increased energy efficiency, however. Automobiles grew bigger and heavier and Detroit perceived a great profit in gadgetry. In the automobile industry the advertising man dominated the engineering man; fins and frills were the only differences year after year. By 1974, the weight of cars was taking its toll on gas mileage. Cars weighing 3,850 to 4,250 pounds were averaging 10.8 miles per gallon and there were a number of other cars getting only 6 miles per gallon.

The industry did not find it necessary to improve the technology, which remained basically the same since the 1940s when such major innovations as automatic transmissions, power brakes and air conditioning had been developed. (Gas-conserving engines and such safety-related items as seat belts, collapsible steering columns and crash-absorption bumpers were all advancements that were developed abroad.)

The level of energy-draining gadgetry was so standardized that nine out of every ten cars had automatic transmissions, with a slightly smaller percentage having power steering. Two out of every three passenger cars came from the factory with air conditioning and a growing number had power brakes. It was an oddity to see a car without a radio. Increasing numbers of cars below Cadillac and Lincoln luxury lines were equipped with other gadgets such as electric windows and doors.

Even competition between economy- and luxury-class cars became confused. In an ever-growing attempt to expand markets, economy cars developed more energy-draining luxurious lines that overlapped with bottom-of-the-line models in luxury classes.

In 1974, the automobile was an all-around expensive tool. The average motorist spent 13.6 cents a mile for a standard car, 10.8 cents a mile for a compact car and 9.4 cents a mile for a subcompact car. The first year of ownership, all the auxiliary expenses—such as repairs, maintenance, accessories, tires, gasoline, depreciation, oil, insurance, garaging, parking, tools, the variety of federal and state registrations, titling and other taxes and fees—cost the average motorist $2,325.32.

The big money the automobile corporations spent on research wasn't for improving the efficiency of the internal combustion engine, or minimizing the metropolitan national air pollution problems (which accounted for as much as 75 percent of the noise and as much as 80 percent of the air pollution in some cities), or for improved safety features to save lives. It was spent instead on styling changes. Each year the industry spends more than $11½ billion for cosmetics and fashion. The money is to make the machine ever more seductive so Detroit can look to ever bigger sales years and see an anticipated 178 million registered vehicles in the United States by 1985.

While it was understood that the automobile had contributed significantly to the demise both of the passenger train and of intra- and inter-urban bus lines, the energy crisis brought new accusations against the monopolistic tactics of the automobile industry.

The charges made before the Senate Antitrust Subcommittee in February 1974, mainly against General Motors, argued that the giant Detroit corporations helped bring about the destruction of public transportation in forty-five cities, including New York, Philadelphia, Baltimore, St. Louis, Oakland, Salt Lake City, Los Angeles and Lincoln, Nebraska. Bradford Snell of the Senate Antitrust Subcommittee charged that, once GM set up its bus business, it deliberately refrained from improving the design; as a result, the "noisy, foul-smelling buses turned earlier patrons of the high speed rail system away from public transit and, in effect, sold millions of private automobiles."

Snell, who spent five years studying the American automobile trusts, in a study entitled "American Ground Transit" summed up the impact of the overall changes:

> General Motors' interlocking control of these competing methods of travel, however, amounts to a serious conflict of interest. The economics are obvious: one bus can eliminate 35 automobiles; one streetcar, sub-

way or rail transit vehicle can supplant 50 passenger cars; one train can displace 1,000 cars or a fleet of 150 cargo-laden trucks. Due to the volume of units displaced, GM's gross revenues are 10 times greater if it sells cars rather than buses, and 25 to 35 times greater if it sells cars and trucks rather than train locomotives. The result was inevitable: a drive by General Motors to maximize profits by wrecking America's rail and bus systems.

We are pouring more than 40 percent of our oil supplies into autos and trucks. If, instead, we used energy efficient trains and mass transit for half of our transport needs, we would save an estimated billion barrels of oil each year, which is more than enough to heat our homes in winter and provide our industries with all the fuel they require.

The contribution of the motorcar to energy waste in the United States cannot be overstated. The internal combustion engine, rubber wheels and the thousands upon thousands of miles of concrete and asphalt symbolize the extravagance of our culture.

The past century has been the most dynamic in the history of man. After rushing through several sources of energy, the uniqueness of petroleum was discovered and its abundance, price and efficiency opened horizons never imagined. It fueled the technological age and was the underlying factor that altered the national social structure. It made the age of machines possible for man, and man became dependent on those machines. It created a hungry, impatient society, pleased with its successes and unable to live without them. It made for a self-indulgent society of big energy spenders and wasters—enamored with itself and self-conscious that it had come too far too fast. Success and affluence had exacted a heavy cost and brought the society to a point of no return.

Wherever one looked or went the excesses of the great energy joyride were on display. They could be observed in overheated and overlighted rooms, in ill-designed buildings, in the orgy of unnecessary travel and in the endemic waste of industries. No one officially certified it, but by the mid-1970s U.S. consumers were at a pinnacle of energy piggery that would probably never again be equaled in human history. In 1974, more than 200 million Americans were using four times more energy per capita than the Japanese, and were burning up more energy for air conditioning alone than 800 million Chinese were using for all purposes.

Energy waste is the great scandal of this generation. It has brought us to the edge of a crisis that will soon force us either to husband our resources or witness the serious disruption of our whole social system.

chapter two

U.S. ENERGY IN PERSPECTIVE: 1800-1945

"Our senses are skeptics, and believe only the impression of the moment, and do not believe the chemical fact that these huge mountain chains are made up of gases and rolling wind. But Nature is as subtle as she is strong. She turns her capital day by day; deals never with dead, but ever with quick subjects. All things are flowing, even those that seem immovable. The adamant is always passing into smoke."

Ralph Waldo Emerson, 1858

By the 1970s energy was so abundant, so omnipresent, in this country that a nation of switch-turners and button-pushers had lost sight of its own swift-moving energy history. Having always thought of ourselves as an independent, oil-rich nation (and being still the foremost oil-producing country in the world), it jarred our complacency to realize that our economy and lifestyle could be cramped by an "oil weapon" brandished by far-away countries.

While the U.S. had modest proven oil reserves, the impact of the Arab embargo taught us that our consumption had far outrun our capacity for production. We also discovered that America did indeed run on oil—and was running dangerously short of adequate supplies. And when the oil-producing countries trebled the price of their product almost overnight, it began to dawn even on the man-in-the-street that maybe an age—the Age of Cheap Energy—was coming to an end.

Yet, until the Arabs acted, U.S. industry had stood like a colossus amid its machines on the assumptions that cheap oil would be available indefinitely, and that if it ran out cheap substitutes could be cranked up to keep the wheels of travel and production turning. Even the energy "experts" were astonished at the rapid change in the petroleum picture: after all, as recently as 1954 we had pumped half the world's oil from our own oil wells and had consumed almost all of it ourselves. Here, then, was a staggering development: serious oil shortages were crippling the country, and we were wholly unprepared for the news that the U.S. oil industry could not rescue us by turning on the taps.

It was a painful shock to be made suddenly aware that the great age of technology had feet of clay—that cheap oil, not technical wizardry, was the dynamo behind our incomparable progress. Yet, this was clearly a major, inescapable conclusion: we had overreached ourselves, and we had been moving at such a giddy pace we had forgotten our own energy history—had even forgotten that oil was, in fact, an exhaustible resource.

Looking at all the energy-driven mechanical marvels of the present, it was easy to forget that the wood-fired steamboat, the mule-drawn barge, and the water-powered grist mill and factory played an important part in the life of America only a little more than a century ago. In the 1850s, the "oil" that was a vital part of the national economy was not petroleum and did not come out of the ground. It was a precious oil for lamps that was captured after a chase in sailing ships on the high seas and processed from the body of a whale. Faded from memory, as well, was the period when "gas" was squeezed from coal to light the lamps of the cities.

Our modern system brings power to people in an instant. Flip a switch and there is light. Turn a dial and there is heat or cool air or a bevy of energy-slaves to do our bidding. Press the ignition and time and space are left quickly behind. Absorbed in this climate-controlled, high-speed, mobile present, it is easy to forget the long, slow process of millions of years which created the irreplaceable fossil fuels—coal and petroleum—which make up 95 percent of our energy today. Until less than ninety years ago, most of our energy came not from this precious debris of ancient plants but directly from the sun (food calories), the driving power of a river, or the force of wind power—or the short-term storage of sun energy in a tree that was cut and split for firewood.

Greek mythology would have it that energy was stolen from the gods by Prometheus and given to man in the form of fire. In addition, Prometheus, who was cruelly punished by the gods for giving a possession suitable for gods alone to mere men, was also credited with giving mortals the technique to forge the elements of what we call civilization from the first flames.

Whether from Prometheus, from a searing bolt of lightning or from a primitive man fashioning stone implements in dry grass, man discovered fire and so changed human history. Whatever the date of the first man-made fire, it altered the world permanently. Once he learned how to control it, primitive man had light, heat, and a weapon against darkness, cold, and the unknown.

Beyond the initial discovery (and fire remained the basic means of energy conversion through the ages) the keys to civilization were the manner in which energy was harvested and how it was used.

Until the unlocking of the atom's nucleus—a mere blink of recorded time ago—all the usable energy of the earth had come from the sun. The rays of the sun warm our bodies and bring light to our days. Radiant energy heats the skin of the earth in uneven patterns and sets up thermal winds in the sky and currents in the oceans. Sun energy also is the force of the hydrologic cycle. The evaporative heat of the sun lifts moisture to the skies to begin the great cycle of water that is the authentic greening agent of this blue planet.

The most important conversion of solar energy occurs in the photosynthetic process. Given the presence of some chlorophyll, some carbon dioxide, and a little water, the cells of green plants capture and store the

radiant energy of the sun in the form of carbohy-
drates—the food that sustains all plant and animal
life.

Those who cultivate crops are really capturing the
energy of the sun. In the growing process, solar
energy is converted into protein and stored in the
kernel of hard grains. When these grains are dried
and properly stored, this nutritious energy of the sun
can be accumulated and used by Homo sapiens in
the long period between harvests.

Some ten thousand years ago, neolithic man turned
from his nomadic hunting and food-gathering ways
and learned to cultivate crops systematically. This
technique of capturing and storing solar energy in the
kernel of grain was a significant moment for the human family. From this point, man was freed from
the ritual of hunting and food gathering. Like all
other forms of animal life, he had been forced to
spend all his waking hours in the precarious pursuit
of game or wild-growing fruits and grains. Now he
could cultivate and store food. He could settle in one
place and begin forming villages, towns and eventually civilizations. Inevitably, the first major civilizations grew up in fertile areas where the domestication
of animals and cultivation of grain thrived.

The process whereby solar energy is converted
into crops—particularly hard grains such as corn,
wheat, barley, sesame, millet and rice—remains as
much a concern of man in the 1970s as it was to the
first neolithic farmers thousands of years ago. The
harvest outlook for American corn and wheat each
year is a matter of international concern. We are

one of the few nations still producing food surpluses in a famine-threatened world, and the capture of protein by farming remains the industry which must always take precedence over all other productive pursuits.

Our fossil fuels are solar energy captured and converted by vegetation on the earth's surface many millennia ago. Thus, the massive coal beds of the world were formed from marshy vegetation growing in slowly submerging swampland some 300 million years ago during the Carboniferous period of the Paleozoic era. Overlying deposits and the folding of the earth covered the decaying vegetation and, through a slow process, that long-dead plant life became coal and oil.

Only recently have the fossil fuels become major sources of energy in the United States. Until 1885, over half of the energy used in this country was short-term solar energy harnessed by burning wood, using falling water, and catching the power of the wind itself in sails and windmills. These were the early mechanical slaves of man—and they combined with the muscles of man and beasts to perform the work of a society that was trying to industrialize itself.

Wood was the dominant energy source during the first century of our history as a nation. It came from the vast forests that once covered most of the country. There used to be a saying that a squirrel could travel through the trees from the Atlantic coast to the Mississippi River without ever touching the ground. By 1850, 90 percent of the fuel consumed in the

country was wood, and it continued to be the predominant form of energy until after the Civil War,
when coal began to make inroads. Even at the turn
of the century, when coal captured first place, Americans still burned as much wood as we had fifty years
previously, and wood contributed 20 percent of the
energy consumed.

Most of the wood that was burned in the United
States was used by individuals to heat homes, and by
small industries, such as the maple syrup, tobacco and
meat industries. Settlers moving west had to clear
large tracts of virgin forest for farmland and often
destroyed the felled trees in large bonfires. There was
never a thought of a shortage of wood. What wasn't
available from clearing fields was just across the
stream or on the side of the hill. Trees were an
obstacle. They cluttered fields needed for pasturing
cattle or growing crops and hindered travel and the
building of communities. Cutting down a tree was—
as with many "modern" subdividers—a public service.

The burning of wood in large, open fireplaces to
heat nineteenth-century homes was perhaps one of
the earlier examples of energy waste. Although wood-
burning stoves were much more efficient in capturing
the heat from a stick of wood, they were incon-
venient to transport to the back country. The average
family needed a prodigious amount of wood. Just
prior to the Civil War, for example, the average
family annually consumed a stack of wood seventy
feet long, eight feet high and four feet wide.

Maintaining such a large supply of wood was obviously a major chore. Usually, the task was assigned to younger members of the family: they had to see that the wood boxes were filled by the kitchen stove and at the fireplaces. They sustained the fire in much the same way that primitive man had. When it was cold, heat still came from one spot, and the family gathered in the flickering glow for warmth and companionship. President Roosevelt shrewdly invoked this tradition when he wanted to reassure the nation during the depths of the Great Depression by calling his radio speeches "fireside chats," for even in the 1930s most homes used fireplaces or woodstoves. To millions of Americans, the president seemed to be present in their living rooms, conversing about common concerns in the trusted atmosphere of a shared hearth.

Besides its abundant supplies of wood, nineteenth-century America was very dependent upon wind energy and water power. Just as in England, the first mechanized factories were in the textile industry. With cotton the dominant industry in the South, with plantations across the countryside soaking up the rays of the sun and converting them into natural fibers, Eli Whitney's invention of the cotton gin in 1793 provided the mechanical means of separating the seeds from the fiber. In the North, the water-powered cotton mill, utilizing a principle developed by the Greeks in about 300 B.C., made its appearance along the stream banks of New England villages.

The first watermill in the United States was built

in Waltham, Massachusetts, in 1813 by Francis Cabot Lowell. In 1832, Lowell and his investors created a thriving textile center at the junction of the Merrimack and Concord Rivers. Soon water-powered factories spread throughout the rural northeast and mid-Atlantic regions of the country. The mills were adapted to process wool, paper and cotton; they also performed the more traditional job of grinding grain. Until the first use of a steam boiler in a Salem, Massachusetts, cotton mill in 1847, these factories were all powered by falling water, even though James Watt's steam engine had been in existence since 1760.

Watermills, windmills and sailing vessels provided most of the harnessed energy of the country until after the Civil War. At midcentury, almost two-thirds of the horsepower used in the manufacture and transportation of goods was produced by the energy of rushing water or blowing wind.

Of course, the most venturesome energy industry in the United States during this period was whaling. Sailing ships from the Massachusetts ports of Nantucket and New Bedford searched the oceans for whales from colonial days until the close of the Civil War. At first, the whales, with their valuable oil stored in fatty layers of blubber just under the skin, were in plentiful supply along the New England coast. But soon they became harder to find, and whaling ships were often hunting and processing whale blubber on the seas for months. Near the end of the whaling era, ships from the United States were searching for the scarce whales as far away as the coast of Japan and in the frigid polar waters. Whale oil was valuable as fuel for lamps and as lubricants, but the increasing cost of whaling and the scarcity of whales sent this romantic industry into decline.

Even though the United States has proved to be one of the coal-rich nations of the world, we did not use it to any extent until about 1830. Not that the techniques of mining coal were unknown: some of the earliest Americans had used coal several centuries before the Europeans. The Hopi Indians in the Southwest, for instance, had used it to heat their homes and make pottery almost a thousand years ago.

Coal mining methods, including the automatic mine pump, had been exploited in Europe before the sixteenth century. In England, where wood was not plentiful, there was a well-established coal industry by 1700. In the United States, however, the superabundance of wood created attitudes similar to the modern attitudes toward oil—no one could imagine running out of it. Anyway, practical men asked, why develop a new source of energy when windmills and waterpowered factories were humming along quite nicely?

The first steamboats and railroad locomotives in the United States were powered by wood, and it remained their principal fuel until the 1870s. During his travels in America, Alexis de Tocqueville observed the steamboat *Louisville* on the Mississippi in 1831 and wrote:

The Louisville on which we are sailing, weighs about
400 tons. It costs 50,000 dollars to build; it is not expected to last more than four years. The fresh water
navigation, the snags and all the other dangers of the
Mississippi reduce the life of ships that ply this river
to that short period (on the average).

The price of wood (average) on the banks of the Mississippi is 2 dollars a cord. The boat consumes 30
cords a day. That makes the expense reach 60 dollars.

Coal, of course, was far more efficient—one-half
ton of coal provided the energy of two tons of wood
at one-half the cost and took up less space. But wood
had its advantages, and both coal and wood continued as competing sources of fuel for steam engines
until after the Civil War. Then cost and supply
factors tipped the competitive balance permanently
in favor of coal.

In the last half of the nineteenth century, the
production and consumption of coal increased dramatically. Between 1850 and 1900, coal production
doubled every ten years, as the total coal output
increased over thirty times from 8.4 million tons
to 269 million tons.

The reason for coal's upsurge was the great boom
in railroad building. In 1830, Peter Cooper invented
the first steam locomotive capable of drawing a train
of cars, making it feasible to link remote parts of
the vast American continent into a cohesive nation,
greatly shortening the travelling time for passengers
and freight and vastly improving the national communications network. The national capital was no

longer a tedious horseback-ride of days or weeks away. It was now possible to build a nation, and the country was united and grew and prospered along the rail lines as this faster, cheaper mode of transportation increased the movement of people and the flow of goods. Factories, granaries, refineries, slaughterhouses, meat packing plants, and many other forms of industry and commerce gathered around railroad centers as new national markets developed. Energy consumption increased, doubled and then redoubled.

Railroad construction had begun in the United States in 1830; by 1860, the nation's railroad network exceeded 30,000 miles. After the Civil War, the building boom was on: from 1860 to 1880, the amount of track tripled to 90,000 miles, and the demand for coal for steel production and boiler fuel increased accordingly. By 1870, coal had replaced wood as the major source of fuel for railroads.

The country was on the move. Chicago, a city with a uniquely favorable geographic location, became the terminal point for a number of rail lines and the transportation center for the nation's rich Midwestern wheat and corn farmlands, the iron ore ranges of Minnesota, the lumber mills of Wisconsin and cotton from the South. In addition livestock from all over the country made Chicago the butcher and meat processor for the nation.

Other cities at the crossroads of busy rail lines, while not nearly as successful as Chicago, nevertheless boomed and prospered as the nation keyed its economy and communications to rail. At first, rail travel, like most early forms of transportation, was primitive and uncomfortable. Over the years, however, it improved dramatically and by the turn of the century was efficient, comfortable and often elegant. It inspired generations of small boys to dream about working for the railroads some day, or travelling to distant cities in the quiet luxury of a Pullman or enjoying a gracious dinner in a carefully appointed dining car.

There is a special "something" about railroad travel that can't be experienced in any other form of long-distance transit. The jet plane, which makes up the bulk of modern long-distance travelling, is an impressive machine, sleek, beautiful and powerful in its roaring, seemingly effortless takeoffs and landings, but it doesn't inspire the passion the train did.

Riding across country on a train provided time to dream in the comforting chatter of the rails and the restful sway of the cars. Out the window was an entire universe at a glance: intriguing-looking small towns; summer fields of wheat; lonely deserts where an animal could be seen lurking in the shadows; a farmhouse, its light shining warmly under an evening snowfall. The imagination could have free reign: "Someday I'll visit that town, walk those fields, sleep alone in that desert and share a winter's evening in that farmhouse." Violent storms could rage and howl outside the coach window, but the train rolled obliviously on, its passengers unconcerned, viewing the wonders.

Although the motorcar and truck eventually moved in on the railroad, luring away its passengers and freight until only a shabby image of a once-proud memory remained, the autos and trucks couldn't replace the romance the railroads had created. Nor could they obliterate the impact the railroad had on writers who grew up in small towns where the wailing train whistle in the night and the friendly clatter of the train wheels on rails symbolized a different way of life, exotic cities and unique opportunities. For Thomas Wolfe, William Saroyan, and a host of other American writers, the image of the train was an intrinsic part of their early dreams of freedom, travel, and success—the whole romantic promise of America embodied in their later writings.

The expansion of the railroads spurred huge increases in demands for steel for rails, new locomotives and other equipment. By 1885, principally because of the railroads and the iron and steel industry, coal became the source of more than half the energy in the United States.

The growth of the use of coal in manufacturing and transportation as well as home heating would continue until after World War I. By the turn of the century, coal-powered locomotives were steaming across America, carrying produce, products and passengers over 193,000 miles of track.

In 1907, coal reached the peak of its contribution to the national energy budget, providing 78 percent of the country's energy needs. It fueled the soaring industrial expansion of the late 1800s and early 1900s —and it changed the character and face of the nation.

Coal consumption and the use of steel grew

together. American steel production, only 20,000 tons in 1879, surpassed the British output with 6 million tons in 1895 and reached 1 million tons before 1900—thus enabling the United States to become one of the major manufacturing nations in the world at the turn of the century. The exploitation of rich deposits of coal and petroleum made this country the most powerful of the Big Power nations of the twentieth century.

The industrial expansion concentrated in the cities around rail and shipping centers and began attracting people to urban America. Young men from the farms and immigrants—mainly from Southern and Eastern European countries—poured into the cities in search of the advertised higher-paying factory jobs and greater opportunities for upward mobility. And the cities felt the strain of accommodating immigrant populations, with their strange languages and foreign ways and, above all, their poverty. The new arrivals clustered in makeshift and rundown communities near the factories, and the heavy smoke and soot of the production processes hung in an ugly pall over the cities. Suffering under the strain of unrest and air pollution, cities lost much of their attractiveness. The more affluent urban dwellers began to drift to the outer perimeters of the city, giving rise to a new American dream of a home with a lawn, where the air was fresh and pure.

Another energy breakthrough occurred in 1879, when Thomas Alva Edison invented the electric light bulb. He subsequently developed a system of electrical distribution and the concept of a central station electrical power plant. Some cities built dams and used water power to turn the new turbines, but coal became the dominant power source for the new electric power industry. Electricity was rapidly adopted, and by 1920 electric motors accounted for more than half of the total installed horsepower in factories, compared to less than 5 percent in 1900.

By the end of World War I, the country had reached the zenith in its appetite for coal—651 million tons. Coal was the great workhorse; more than one-quarter of the total consumed in the nation fed the boilers of the railroads, and large amounts were used in homes for newly developed central heating.

In the 30 years from roughly 1920 to 1950, "king coal" was dethroned by petroleum for one simple reason—oil in nearly every way was a much better fuel. Once big oilfields were discovered and the techniques of refining and transporting oil and natural gas were perfected, a dramatic new energy potential was at hand. These fuels were cleaner, more versatile, easier to handle—and, most important, abundant and cheap. As a result, they wrought vast changes in transportation, in industry, and in the source of energy for individual homes.

Since the end of World War I, the use of coal in the United States has been gradually declining. Just as the rapid advance of the coal industry was fostered by the expansion of the railroads and their growing need for steel and boiler fuel, so the decline of coal stemmed from the decline of the railroads and the rise of the automobile and truck industry.

After World War I, expansion of rail lines slowed down, as did freight and passenger business. Coal diminished even more in importance with the development of the diesel-powered train after World War II. Oil also replaced coal in ships, which had been heavy users of coal.

With the building of vast pipeline networks, oil and gas also swiftly took over a substantial share of the market in commercial and residential space heating after World War II, dramatically altering a way of life.

Heating a home with coal, although more efficient and less complicated than heating it with wood, nevertheless, required constant attention. Even though most homes were by then centrally heated, the coal furnance was an awesome thing that demanded care and cleaning. Vents and doors took the coal furnace was an awesome thing that de-filthy coal bin with a chute coming in from the street and a short-handled shovel were nearby. Someone had to feed this monster, keep it functioning and clean up the ashes and melted clinkers, which were shoveled into buckets and lugged from the cellar.

With natural gas or heating oil as a home fuel, the household could skip all the old chores. The burning process was cleaner and quieter; the gas furnace, where used, was hidden and forgotten. The heat was there, but almost the only thing the family had to do to ensure a steady supply was pay the bill.

With the increased use of oil, the only area where coal held its own, even in the postwar period, was in the production of electricity. By 1970, half of the nation's 3,000 power plants were coal-fired and consumed about 300 million tons of coal. This was almost a tenfold increase over the amount of coal used to generate electricity in 1920.

The discovery of oil and its development as a versatile fuel and raw material was an outgrowth of unprecedented U.S. industrial pioneering. The oil was always there—learning to put it to use was the problem. During the 1700s, the Seneca Indians used blankets to soak up oil that floated on the tops of creeks in western Pennsylvania. They then used it for various medicinal purposes.

When oil seeping from the earth began to foul wells in Allegheny County, Pennsylvania, that had been drilled to capture brine for salt, American enterprise built on the Indian experience. This otherwise useless product, which was ruining the salt, was bottled and huckstered as an all-purpose elixir. "Rock Oil" from the springs and wells of Pennsylvania thus became an early medical nostrum, promising health and comfort to thousands during the early 1850s.

During this same period, the search had begun for animal and vegetable oils to supplement whale oil as fuels to light the nation's lamps. By the mid-nineteenth century, many urban areas were able to use gaslight in commercial buildings and a coal-derivative in the homes of the very wealthy. How-

ever, supplies were scarce, and a search continued
for a cheaper, more profitable means of bringing
light to American homes. This led to the "squeez-
ing" of coal-oil or kerosene from coal.

In 1857, E. L. Drake decided to apply the primitive salt-brine drilling technique to the search for
oil. On August 27, 1859, at a depth of less than 70
feet, Drake's drilling crew made the first oil strike,
in Titusville, Pennsylvania. It was not a geyser, or
even much of a gusher, but it was a discovery of a
remarkable energy source that would change America irrevocably.

Soon this area of Pennsylvania was dotted with
oil derricks and crude rigs. Speculators, fortune
hunters and the full complement of characters that
rush to any boom town swarmed in. A gusher would
come in and a poor farmer became wealthy. Another
man would produce nothing but dry holes, or perhaps an initial strike that could not be controlled
and soon fizzled out. Production at first fluctuated
widely, and, with little initial ability to regulate a
well or store its output, the black stuff flowed uncol-
lected on the ground and into the waterways. Enough
oil was coming in, however, for it soon to glut the
market. In the two-year period from 1860 to 1862,
overproduction dropped prices per barrel from about
$20 to 10 cents.

With the first oil well producing almost accidently,
the necessary technical advancements to make oil
into a commercial industry were developed on the
run. Within a few decades oil attracted resourceful,

ruthless entrepreneurs and the basic technology—drilling, collecting, piping, refining, storing, transporting and bringing the product to markets—was mastered. There were great financial opportunities in this new, chaotic industry for the strong man who could put together an organization capable of monopolizing or dominating each aspect of oil production—from the capital investment to the drilling of the well itself to the delivery of the end product directly to the consumer. Such a man was John D. Rockefeller, and his organization was Standard Oil.

Rockefeller invested in an oil refinery in 1863. Two years later he bought out one of his partners and was on his way to a commanding position in the industry. Standard Oil was soon making barrels for its own use and had its own railroad cars. By 1874, a subsidiary was in the pipeline business. In 1888, Standard Oil built the first steam tanker in the U.S. and began its ocean fleet. By 1890, the company was delivering kerosene to its domestic consumer in a fleet of tank wagons. And in the late 1890s, Standard Oil controlled the entire production of the Lima, Ohio, and Indiana oil fields that had been opened in the previous decade.

Within the first ten years of the Titusville oil strike and the opening of the Appalachian fields, oil production had increased from 500,000 barrels to over 5 million barrels a year. By 1895, crude oil production had again made a tenfold jump to more than 52 million barrels annually.

Throughout the early years of the oil industry, the

major product derived from crude oil was kerosene for lighting purposes. Until just after the turn of the century, more than 50 percent of refinery output was kerosene, a significant portion of which was exported to foreign markets by the aggressive Rockefeller organization.

Kerosene was a superior source of illumination. It was cheaper, more available and a brighter source of light than the animal or vegetable oil or candles then in use. Also, it was safer and less odorous than camphene, an explosive, foul-smelling lamp oil distilled from a combination of turpentine and alcohol.

One of the unique characteristics of petroleum was its versatility: it offered oil men manifold opportunities to open up ever-widening markets for an ever-growing family of petroleum products. The composition of the crude oil in the Ohio-Indiana fields was found to be high in fuel oils, a discovery that stimulated a drive to make inroads into the transportation and industry fuel markets then dominated by coal.

By 1900, the use of petroleum as a fuel for electric and industrial boilers was on the increase. In 1909, nearly half the total crude oil production was directly consumed for heat and power. Nearly one-quarter was used to power railroads in California and the Southwest, where cheap coal was not available. Another quarter was used in manufacturing. By this time, the focus of crude oil production had shifted to the giant new oil fields of Texas, Oklahoma and California.

During the first quarter of the twentieth century,

most petroleum was used for boiler fuel, with two-thirds of the crude oil and half of the refinery production allocated for that purpose in the 1920s. However, the percentage of a 42-gallon barrel of oil that was refined into residential and commercial heating oil declined steadily as the motorcar and the internal combustion engine—with their insatiable appetite for gasoline—became prominent.

Early in the century, the automobile was hardly a threat to the efficient network of electric railways and electrified trolleys which served U.S. cities and connected the main urban areas of the country. With only about eight thousand cars on a meager system of poor roads in 1900, the automobile was little more than a rich man's plaything.

Henry Ford changed all that when, in 1908, he began mass producing automobiles on an assembly-line process. His Model-T came on the market at a price of $900. It was the only model he planned to produce and came in a variety of colors "so long as it is black."

The success of the Model-T exceeded Ford's dreams. By 1913, the number of registered automobiles surpassed the million mark, and three years later the increased market and improved production techniques brought the price down to $345. A large segment of America's population could now afford a car, and by the 1920s registration again nearly doubled. Ford was so successful that by 1927 more than half of the more than 20 million cars on the road were Model-T's.

Although automobile sales declined slightly during the Great Depression, the rush to the road revived, and just before World War II motor vehicle registrations reached 32.5 million. Following the war, sales rose to dizzy heights, and by the middle of the 1950s the number of registered vehicles had doubled again. Thus, between 1918 and 1955, the number of automobiles increased eightfold. However, as long trips became commonplace, the consumption of gasoline multiplied even faster, and by the mid-fifties motor vehicles were using nearly twenty times the amount of fuel that they had consumed about forty years previously. Americans had become more dependent on the automobile and used it with greater frequency—for shopping, riding, commuting from points farther and farther from their jobs.

To keep up with the increased demand for gasoline, more and more crude oil was needed, and refinery production was increasingly directed towards fulfilling the requirements of this growing market. At the turn of the century, only about 14 percent of the crude oil barrel was gasoline. By 1913, the process of breaking down the complex, heavier molecules of petroleum into the simpler, lighter molecules of gasoline had been discovered and exploited to increase the yield of gasoline from each barrel.

The demand for petroleum products was also increased by the growing use of these fuels in farm machines, airplanes and railroad locomotives. Diesel locomotives became dominant after World War II, and jet airplanes began to streak across the sky. By

1950, some one billion barrels of fuel—nearly half of all the petroleum used in the United States—were consumed by the internal combustion engine.

The existence of natural gas had been known in this country since colonial times (sometimes it was encountered in the drilling of water or salt-brine wells). At first it was considered an unwanted by-product and burned off in the oil fields. It was the development of high-pressure, long-distance gas pipelines which made natural gas a primary fuel that rivaled crude oil.

By the 1880s, the first high-pressure gas line connected Chicago with the natural gas fields of Indiana. However, as the oil industry moved west and south and opened up the Texas, California and Oklahoma fields in the first decade of this century, more than 90 percent of the natural gas was lost. Improvements in the design and manufacture of pipe extended the range and by the end of the 1920s, it was possible to deliver gas up to one thousand miles.

The use of natural gas as a fuel increased significantly after World War II. More pipelines were constructed, and because gas was a cleaner, more efficient fuel, it rapidly replaced coal in homes and industry in the 1950s and '60s. By the 1970s, half the nation's 63 million homes were heated by natural gas (the bulk of the remainder by oil).

In retrospect, it was sheer abundance that changed our whole outlook toward energy. As the annual production-consumption curves spiraled steadily upward, as our proven domestic oil reserves grew—and as the big U.S. international oil companies made extraordinary new oil strikes in all parts of the world, discoveries we arrogantly counted as expansions of "our" oil, the conviction deepened that the Petroleum Age was just beginning and would continue well into the twenty-first century.

The U.S. *was* the predominant oil nation when World War II ended. We *were* an oil-rich country. Our petroleum prices *were* incredibly cheap. And one could plausibly argue that we could command whatever energy we needed for the foreseeable future. However, most of the assumptions that were rooted in this bullish outlook were illusions—and these myths and misconceptions would cause us to plunge impulsively into an awesome spree that would consume resources we should have saved, and propel us into a long-term energy crisis in the 1970s.

chapter three

THE SWIFT TRANSITIONS
OF THE PETROLEUM AGE

"The looming energy crisis in America is not serious,
it is catastrophic. America has been burning up its oil
and gas supplies to support its extravagant lifestyle
as if there were no tomorrow."

—Robert O. Anderson
Chairman,
Atlantic Richfield Oil Co.
1973

The Petroleum Age has entered its decline. There
are no meaningful substitutes for oil in sight. This,
stated starkly, is the energy crisis. It is a major
development, one that will change the course of our
history and dominate our lives for several decades.

Nineteen seventy-four was a year of confusion
about the energy crisis—and for legitimate reasons.
The issue is so enormously complex that the facts
themselves are in dispute. The American people are
bewildered because they have taken energy for
granted for the last three decades. An overwhelming
majority assumed science had "solved" the energy
problem; others were confident that powerful inter-

national leaders would warn us if there were a threat of serious fuel shortages.

This complacency was shattered by the events of the winter of 1974. Even as the realization grew that the Arab oil embargo had only exacerbated existing shortages, most Americans refused to see the crunch as a long-term issue. How, they asked, could the world's number one oil-producing and -using nation—a nation that had just watched its automobile industry set a new record for production—run out of oil? How could the country which put men on the moon find itself with empty gas pumps and push-buttons that did not produce instant power?

There were no simple answers to such questions. The real answers were rooted in the mistakes and misguided policies which prevailed during the era of galloping growth that began after World War II. It was these policies and an assortment of myths, illusions and mistaken assumptions that produced the great energy joyride and brought the country to the edge of major economic dislocations in the early months of 1974. One had to go back to the aftermath of World War II to understand the scope and momentum of American energy superconsumption.

The Big Postwar Surge

For nearly all the great nations sucked into its vortex, World War II was a vast disaster: cities and industries were damaged or destroyed, national economies were crippled, vital resources were wasted, nations were decimated, and military and civilian casualties by the million were totaled. Geography made the United States the one exception to this rule. On V-J Day in August 1945, our cities were unscathed and our industrial plant was intact, in high gear—and ready for conversion to peacetime production. We not only became a world power, but a superpower. The conclusion of the war also marked the end of a long period of lean living and Spartan sacrifices which had spanned the years from the onset of the Great Depression in 1929 to 1945. These years, in which incomes were meager and goods were scarce, had created an enormous pent-up demand for housing, autos and products of every description. Fortunately, our postwar full-employment policy worked, and unprecedented economic growth gave U.S. citizens the purchasing power to buy the things they had coveted. It also primed an appetite for things they never knew they wanted.

Our country's pioneering petroleum industry was able and anxious to play a paramount role in the new consumer-oriented economy. The oil industry had performed spectacularly during the war. Almost singlehandedly it had fueled the war machine of the Allies, and in the process had widened its experience in pipeline technology, in the operation of huge fleets of ocean-going tankers and in using petroleum to create such products as synthetic rubber.

The oilmen had always known petroleum was a versatile resource, and now they had a chance to prove it in peacetime. They were ready to preempt much of the home-heating market by building new natural gas pipelines to all parts of the country; they were prepared to enlarge their refinery capacity to produce the quantities of home-heating oil, diesel oil and boiler fuels that would sharply shrink the contribution of the coal industry and the railroads to our economic life; and they would soon provide new markets for their raw materials by creating a petrochemical industry that would use huge amounts of oil and gas to produce medicines, plastics, fertilizers, and thousands of new chemical products. As for the automobile, the oil industry was as anxious as Detroit to see Henry Ford's dream of an auto for every family come to fruition.

The boom days of petroleum lay ahead, and the leaders of this ambitious industry were in an uncommonly bullish frame of mind in 1945. Theirs was the world's number-one "can-do" capitalist enterprise. They had put the U.S. in a position where it was producing and using well over half of the world's oil. In addition they had sent teams of technicians to such far-off places as the Middle East and South America, where they discovered some of the world's giant oil fields and secured them under favorable long-term concession leases.

This was an intoxicating time for U.S. oilmen. True, an oil glut existed, and they saw the need to generate increases in consumption as their big problem. But they were certain the petroleum age was still in its early stages and that ways could be found to push consumption to higher and higher levels. Here was a swaggering industry without nay-sayers, and however much their promotional activities might increase future consumption, hardly anyone then doubted there was enough oil to take care of the country's needs well into the twenty-first century.

The facts supported most of this optimism. Drilling activity was at a very high level in the immediate postwar period, and our proven reserves increased every year until 1961. The number of oil and gas wells that were drilled more than doubled, from 24,666 in 1945 to almost 56,000 in 1955. In addition, everyone assumed all of the huge postwar "strikes" in foreign countries were "our" oil—and expanded "our" reserves even further.

Oil did more than light the lamps during the big U.S. energy binge—it turned the wheels everywhere: it was the workhorse that made our "technological miracles" work.

What occurred was an unparalleled explosion of industrial production and materialistic progress. American expectations were elevated as people worked fewer hours and saw their standard of living steadily escalate. The changes and statistics were startling. For example, nearly one-half of U.S. workers had achieved white-collar status by 1955; and in the 20 years after Pearl Harbor, the output of U.S. goods and services grew as much as it had grown in the entire century from 1841 to 1941. The rise in individual affluence was dramatic: in 1940 only slightly more than 3 percent of the population had sufficient income to require them to pay any federal income tax. In 1960 over 48 million people, over half of the adult population, were prosperous enough to be taxpayers. We were also using nearly three times as much energy in 1960 as in 1940, even though our population had increased only 36 percent.

It was a giddy period, so giddy we ignored the role of cheap oil and pretended we were technological supermen. We spoke overbearingly of our "jet age," "age of automation," and "space age"—but none of them would have succeeded had it not been for our superabundance of petroleum. In the twenty years after Pearl Harbor, our energy consumption had trebled, and the experts assured us this was only the beginning. They created the impression that American life was an escalator; all we had to do was to clutch the handrail and encourage the remarkable energy-hungry technologies that were changing our lives.

In fact, nearly all of the principal postwar trends and developments made huge new demands on the growth-minded energy industries. "Bigger is better" was the key tenet of the American business philosophy, and a scale-up in the size of everything from aircraft, cars, highways and high-rise buildings to shopping centers and mining machinery created huge increases in the need for fuel.

The largest permanent increase in fuel consumption resulted from the interdependent development of rural land and the proliferation of automobiles.

Sprawl, we now belatedly realize, was feasible not simply because we were affluent and had an aggressive auto industry, but because cheap land and cheap gasoline and cheap natural gas created a freewheeling way of life that enabled us to build low-density suburban communities and to carve up and sell land by the acre in a vast, one-time orgy of land speculation. The idea that every family should own a separate home on its own private turf was a noble absurdity from the outset—but it worked for a few years thanks to the frantic oil-pumping activities of the petroleum industry.

The energy miscalculation was central. Sprawl was a seemingly rational concept for urbanization at the outset, but it ended by creating a monster that looms as one of the great misjudgments of the postwar period.

In similar fashion, we attributed most of our striking successes in agriculture to advances in agronomy and "modern" farming practices. However, even the astonishing gains in farm production, where most yields were doubled and then redoubled, were attributable to the availability of cheap petroleum. It was petroleum-based fertilizers and enormous savings made possible by increasingly mechanized farming that were crucial. They, too, were an outgrowth of the big pump-out of petroleum.

Measured in terms of money, jobs and GNP, the outcome was a smashing success. Nevertheless, a scale-up of this magnitude had a broad impact on the lifestyles—and sense of values—of the average American.

For example, the auto and truck—and the highway construction juggernaut that subsidized them—made us a "nation on wheels," but the rush to motorized vehicles and the suburbs also disrupted and damaged important personal and social values. The mobility treadmill—convenient and pleasurable as it was part of the time—was as much a curse as a blessing.

We paid a high price for the conventional attributes of progress. As the big engines roared ahead in high gear, unbridled technology had a deadly impact on the overall environment. Across the land, the tentacles of contamination were widening their hold on rivers, estuaries, lakes and watersheds; industrial wastes were fouling workplaces, encroaching on dwellings, and limiting the usefulness of open space, beachlands, parks and wildlife habitats. The results were stark and simple. There was not a single large city that was as livable in 1960 as it had been in 1950. There was not a major river that was as clean as it had been a decade earlier.

Citizen acquiescence in this gigantic consumer barbecue indicated that many of the changes were altering our values. If a statistical measurement of jobs and incomes was the only test, a debasing of personal and public values was inevitable. If the primary goal of life was to own things and be mobile, many of the old values were compromised or foresworn. Traditional community loyalties were weakened, pride in craftsmanship was compromised, and the idea that manufactured goods should be judged primarily by their durability was tossed into the ashcan. Some passed off the problem by repeating the cliché, "You can't stand in the way of progress." And others consoled themselves with the thought that we were now so rich and so clever that these things really didn't matter.

The logic of the postwar growth gospel was crisp and compelling, and it had implications in all areas of life. If bigger was better, then more was better yet! "Multiply and replenish" was no longer just a Biblical dictum; it was a commandment of the National Association of Manufacturers. A new ideology of consumption was abroad. If bulldozing of rich farmlands for suburban homesites rang the GNP cash register and raised the spiral of profits, it was automatically assumed to be in the national interest.

And with each increase of GNP, smugness and self-congratulation also increased. The *New York Herald Tribune*'s financial editor expressed the prevailing business philosophy as the decade of the 1950s closed when he wrote: "If a whole people can be said to wallow in prosperity, Americans will do it in 1960 as, uninhibited, they gluttonously reap the fruits of 183 years of free enterprise."

World Oil Dominance: The Mid-Fifties

No one acknowledged the milestone, but the high-water mark of U.S. global oil supremacy came in the mid-fifties. We still had what amounted to a stranglehold on "free world" oil in the Eisenhower years. If the U.S. had pumped almost exactly half of the oil extracted in the whole world in 1954, we were also using well over half of the internal combustion engines that were operating in the world; we were burning up over half of the gasoline and jet fuel consumed—and we were confidently planning to double and then redouble our consumption of such fuels well before the year 2000.

Our proven petroleum reserves were nearing an all-time high in the mid-fifties, and the initial exploration of the promising continental shelf off Texas and Louisiana offered the promise that they contained "vast " additional reserves.

Except for two unrelated events, it was galloping growth as usual for the energy industries in the fifties. The first was the unveiling of the "Atoms for Peace" program by President Eisenhower in 1955. This new scenario of superabundance was written by prestigious nuclear scientists who assured the country that within a few decades the "peaceful atom" would become an inexhaustible source of clean, cheap energy. This glowing announcement erased any lingering worries of the oilmen. The script for the world's long-term energy transition was written, and it didn't really matter whether we had enough oil to sustain us to 1990 or, say, to 2020. The nuclear panacea gave everyone a comfortable fallback position.

This unfaltering faith that technology had mastered the techniques needed to give us all the energy we would ever need was expressed vigorously in the Rockefeller Panel studies presented in 1958. These bullish reports, prepared by such experts as Dean Rusk, Henry Kissinger, and Arthur Burns, were considered unofficial "white papers" on the American future. They counseled the nation that the Cold War could be lost if we did not further accelerate production and exploit the advantages of technology. Parts of these reports were also written in the glowing ink of superoptimism:

> New technologies, more efficient extraction processes, new uses may open up new worlds. Even now we can discern the outlines of a future in which, through the use of the split atom, our resources of both power and raw materials will be limitless. . . . In the 20th Century the unprecedented acceleration of scientific advance promises that we are only on the threshold of a new age of science. . . . The world may well be on the verge of a major revolution in available energy. Already the proven resources of uranium and thorium, in terms of energy equivalent, are at least 1,000 times the world resources of coal, gas and oil.

The second event was a notable dissent within the oil fraternity. It caused no immediate splash, but it would be something to reckon with in the 1970s, when shocking oil shortages developed. In 1956 Dr. M. King Hubbert, a geologist and geophysicist who worked for Shell Oil Company, published a paper in which he accurately predicted the course of U.S. oil production. He had laboriously developed an original analytical method which enabled him to forecast that potential U.S. oil reserves were more limited than anyone had heretofore suspected and that U.S. production would probably peak out sometime around 1970. At the time, Hubbert's was a lone voice: his bearish prediction was treated by the oilmen of the fifties as a piece of ridiculous pessimism—and Hubbert was dismissed as an oddball.

The Sixties

The energy roller coaster picked up momentum in the 1960s. A production glut was still considered the big problem by the oil industry, and a national campaign was launched to encourage travel and other forms of petroleum consumption. These efforts succeeded far beyond the expectations of the oilmen. Overall growth continued at a 5 percent annual rate —and an oil import quota imposed by the government protected the bulk of the U.S. market for domestic producers. The use of petroleum in such energy-intensive industries as petrochemicals and fertilizers grew at an even steeper rate, and during the 1960s the annual growth rate of gasoline consumption jumped from 2 percent to 6 percent as the U.S. auto population surged by an astonishing 60 percent. (More than 50 percent of the nation's energy growth from 1950 to 1970 was in natural gas. By 1970 it was the second most important source of fuel, supplying one-third of the nation's needs.)

As those who were at the helm of government in the 1960s know all too well, there was then no national energy policy. Or, more precisely, the policy was laissez faire—the oil companies largely decided what was done. For several reasons, energy policy issues were kept out of the political arena. Most importantly, perhaps, the public was content with the low prices charged for gasoline and natural gas. In addition the oilmen had powerful leverage in both major political parties; the government's own petroleum experts in the Interior Department's United States Geological Survey (USGS) misled everyone by publishing "official" estimates of our potential petroleum reserves that were even more optimistic than those of the oilmen; nearly everyone had absolute faith in the nuclear nostrum; and there was a fallback consensus that, if worse came to worst, we could always fill the gaps by importing "our" cheap oil from the countries in the Middle East.

The Seventies

The common global forecast of the energy experts as the 1970s began was that more oil would be consumed in the coming decade than had been consumed in the century-long period since Drake's first oil well in 1859. This was the projection used by the oilmen as they planned our energy future, but, even as they stood back in amazement at the magnitude of their own grandiose arithmetic of expansion, ominous small clouds gathered on the horizon.

Several warning signals appeared at the turn of the decade to mar the sky-is-the-limit expectations of the oilmen:

> U.S. oil production, as Hubbert had predicted, peaked and started to decline in November 1970; and U.S.

proven reserves continued to follow the downward dip he had foretold in the fifties;

U.S. demands for oil were projected to double by 1985 and double again by the year 2000;

the growing gap between U.S. production and consumption required substantial annual increases in foreign imports to prevent crippling shortages from occurring;

Texas (which had long served as the U.S. oil production "surge tank") went to 100 percent production for the first time in forty years;

the highly-touted Prudhoe Bay field in Alaska—the largest oil field (10–12 billion barrels) ever discovered on the North American continent—turned out to have enough oil to supply U.S. needs at current consumption rates for only two and one-half years;

the nuclear power program became highly controversial, and lost its cure-all aura;

and, most alarming of all, world oil consumption reached such a high level that a seller's market developed, and the weak organization of Oil Producing and Exporting Countries (OPEC) was suddenly in the driver's seat and began to raise prices.

From the U.S. perspective, these developments clearly foreshadowed a new era in the history of oil. They were a warning that our whole bloated energy system had become a monster we could not continue to feed; and they showed unmistakably that we had grossly misjudged our potential petroleum reserves and were trying to formulate an ad hoc energy policy without any real agreement on how much oil we had left. In short, all the signs indicated that we were on the threshold of a major energy crisis that would cripple our economy unless programs of retrenchment and conservation were carried out.

It is folly to build our hopes and assumptions on paper energy, or on gigantic undiscovered offshore oil reserves—or on foreign supplies supposedly under the "control" of the U.S.-based international oil companies. Unless we are so outrageously foolhardy as to land the Marines somewhere, we had better reconcile ourselves to the fact that the OPEC countries will continue to charge very high prices for their crude oil.

Yet, despite these disturbing indicators, and despite the shock-wave impact of the Arab embargo, official Washington pretended that the crisis was a "one-time, short-term" problem. Richard Nixon's energy thinking obviously froze somewhere in the 1950s. If anything, he was more bullish than the oilmen, an unwavering supporter of the nuclear nostrum, seemingly unfamiliar with the ethic of conservation. He appeared to hold the view that U.S. patterns of consumption are sacrosanct, and had no apparent doubts that the U.S. oil industry could find and "dig out" the staggering amounts of additional petroleum we are counting on for the next decades. Even Shell Oil Company president Harry Bridges recognized the fallacy of such logic when he later stated that there "is not a hope in hell that discoveries anywhere in the world will replace the Middle East."

Any country will flounder if its leaders base a vital national policy on misjudgment and illusions. It is increasingly clear we cannot come to grips with our energy crisis as long as our policymaking ignores hard truths and is dominated by myths. In 1974 we were, for example, making extravagant consumption plans for the future and operating on the illusion that we are still the world's petroleum powerhouse when, in fact, we were slowly becoming a have-not nation. Likewise, our Washington planners were pretending we would soon discover vast offshore oil reserves on our continental shelves which would keep the pipelines flowing, when no one really knows how much oil is out there. Many economists, who nurture their own set of illusions, were acting as though much higher prices for crude oil would act as a kind of magic suction-pump which would increase the output of U.S. oil wells overnight and thus bring supply and demand into balance. High enough prices always bring supply and demand into balance, often at the cost of enormous dislocations, inflation, loss of jobs, and unavailability of goods. And finally, the big oilmen, who clung to the old myths that served them in the past, were continuing to prate that if we let them make enough money they would find the oil and eliminate the shortages.

Our predicament will continue to worsen as long as we continue to ground our policies on such self-deception. An historic blunder has occurred. We are making an oil policy without deciding how much oil we have left. We are asking our oil industry to make big increases in production, without knowing whether it is practicable for them to do so. We are assuming that "alternate sources" can be turned on like a tap, without evaluating the enormous obstacles to big achievements in production. Indeed, the full scope of our self-deception was evident in the winter of 1974 when President Nixon was boasting of our upcoming "energy independence," while sending his Secretary of State as a shuttling supplicant to persuade the Arab leaders to turn on their taps and rescue the floundering U.S. economy. The sobering truth is that our energy position is now so exposed that Arab oil is our "ace in the hole" for the remainder of the 1970s.

Of all these public exercises in self-deception, however, the myth that we have vast offshore reserves which can keep the energy carnival going is the most misleading. It does the most to dramatize the folly of our current policies.

Apparently, many oil industry and government officials believe that we can ransack the unexplored regions of our continental shelves and increase the oil output of the United States by as much as 25 percent in the next few years. However, most evidence does not support such bullish hopes, and a more extensive analysis of the available data suggests that it is neither feasible, nor in the long-term national interest, to attempt to launch a "crash" effort on the continental shelves for short-term advantage.

Rapid exploitation of our continental shelves off the Atlantic, Alaskan, Pacific and Gulf shorelines is not feasible because the oil companies lack the funds, the equipment and the necessary lead time to carry out such a staggering short-run program. If American production is to be kept even at its current levels without making an even more drastic drawdown of our modest proven reserves, we must discover at least 4 billion barrels of new oil each year. In our twenty-year search for offshore oil, our most promising shelf area—the supposedly oil-rich Gulf coast—has only produced new reserves averaging one-half billion barrels per year. As all the experts admit, however, drilling for oil along the Atlantic and Alaskan coast-lines poses formidable new engineering obstacles and serious environmental risks. Concern with these prob-lems, and the uncertainty about the extent—if any —of oil and gas reserves in these areas make a com-pelling case for a go-slow approach in these areas.

On what can only be described as flimsy facts, Interior Secretary Rogers C. B. Morton and oil indus-try leaders have assured the country that a great effort to ransack our four continental shelves will yield the enormous increases in oil supplies we need (and have projected) for the next several decades. This is the same glib outlook which got us into trouble in the first place. The extravagant predictions of potential petroleum reserves voiced by the oilmen and boomer geologists in the USGS have misled the country for the past two decades. And now, in a mind-boggling act of faith, we are continuing to construct crucial policies on the sand castles of their discredited "facts."

All of the misleading assumptions and the whole distorted story are summed up in a case study of the dispute over the undiscovered oil resources under the Atlantic continental shelf.

The Atlantic Shelf: A Case Study

In April 1973 news stories appeared about "hot" Atlantic offshore oil prospects. These reports were based on extensive seismic studies carried out on the Atlantic shelf over a six-year period by scientists in the USGS. Such tests revealed the presence of sedimentary basins and possibly promising geologic structures, but they did not provide hard data concerning the amounts or probable presence of oil-bearing stratas. Nevertheless, after evaluating the results, USGS scientists performed their official function and estimated that the Atlantic continental shelf contains a potential 48 billion barrels of oil. This guess—it was no more than that—quickly became transmuted into black, producible oil.

The day after the announcement was made (in early 1974) that offshore leasing was to be vastly expanded, the Secretary of the Interior, USGS figures in hand, informed the Congress that the potential recovery from the Outer Continental Shelf of the United States was a whopping 200 billion barrels of crude oil and about 850 trillion cubic feet of natural gas. On the Atlantic coast alone, Secretary Morton claimed in factual tones, 48 billion barrels of oil and 220 trillion cubic feet of natural gas were available. Spokesmen for the oil industry joined in and assured the country that the threatening oil shortages could be overcome if the oil companies were given quick access to these new provinces.

A more conservative interpretation of the Atlantic

coast seismic studies was presented a few weeks later by Dr. Hubbert. Hubbert is a cautious scientist. To him the USGS Atlantic shelf study was a mere indication ". . . that if sediments of the stated thicknesses do exist, they may *possibly* contain a few billion barrels of oil." He is not a contentious man, but Hubbert felt the language used by his colleagues in the government report showed "a strong bias toward exaggerated estimates"; he also expressed surprise at the forecast that the Atlantic shelf would contain more oil than the shelf off Louisiana and Texas, where a total of less than 10 billion barrels have been discovered in twenty years of drilling. Hubbert is a realist. He believes we should base our national policies only on oil that has been drilled and oil fields that have been scientifically delineated.

Considering the contrast between Hubbert's estimates and those of the Geological Survey "experts," it is not surprising that Congress was confused. And the confusion turned to total bewilderment in late March 1974 when, with no rational explanation for the turn-about, the USGS released "revised estimates" which drastically diminished the nation's offshore energy potentials and pulled the rug out from under Secretary Morton, with his optimistic plans. The "revised estimates" were a rather astounding scale-down from the previous predictions. For example, the 200-billion-barrel total for the continental shelves was reduced to 100 billion, and overnight the highly advertised 48 billion barrels on the Atlantic shelf shrank to a mere 15 billion. This breathtaking depletion at one stroke punctured the arrogant optimism that was the foundation of the administration's energy policy.

But, even if they concede for the purpose of argument that Hubbert is right and the Petroleum Age is in its decline, the optimists still contend we can keep up the momentum of the energy binge. The new solution, we are told, is a crash program to develop the nation's "alternate energy sources." And true to form, a new attempt is made to overwhelm those searching for facts by using astronomical numbers to describe the other fossil fuel resources—coal and shale. There has always been a strong element of hyperbole in the language of the oilmen. The most common adjective used to depict U.S. petroleum resources is "boundless"; all new oil fields are invariably referred to as "vast"; and Alaska's oil potential is usually described as either "limitless" or "fabulous." U.S. coal resources are commonly described as enough to fill "all of our energy needs for five hundred years." And the impression is conveyed that the great beds of subterranean rock that constitute Colorado's "vast" oil shale reserves can readily be turned into great new rivers of oil.

However, the easy energy days are over. The development of the so-called alternate sources is a very difficult and enormously important undertaking.

U.S. PETROLEUM MILESTONES

Pioneer Period

1859   First U.S. oil well drilled

1905   High tide of Rockefeller's Standard Oil Trust: petroleum supplies only 10% of U.S. energy

1925   U.S. produces 71% of the world's oil

1930   Conditions of glut: oil sells for 10¢ a barrel

1945   U.S. uses 4½ million barrels of oil a day while supplying 70% of allied war needs.

Golden Age of Oil

1949   U.S. is an oil-exporting country

1953   U.S. oil companies account for about half of world oil production

1954   U.S. pumps half of the world's oil from domestic fields and consumes nearly all of it in this country

1955   U.S. has 20% of the estimated world crude oil reserves

Maturity and Decline

1961   U.S. proven reserves reach a peak and begin to decline

1970   U.S. production peaks and begins to decline

1973   U.S. imports 38% of the oil it uses

1973   U.S. annually consumes about 30% of the world oil supply

1973   U.S. has only 5% of proven world reserves

chapter four

ENERGY ILLUSIONS
AND ENERGY ALTERNATIVES

"In down-to-earth reality, a series of bottlenecks unprecedented for peacetime is hindering plans for tap-
ping additional sources of energy. The obstructions
range from a labyrinthine array of restrictive government regulations to shortages of such necessities as oil-
drilling equipment, coal hopper cars and water for
fuel-processing plants. . . . High prices for oil and
coal add a compelling inducement. But patriotism
and profit lures alone can't bring forth fuel."

—*The Wall Street Journal*
May 9, 1974

"Technological wizardry is not an end in itself. It is
desirable only if it makes for human welfare, and this
is the test that any tool ought to be made to pass . . .
a technological masterpiece may be a human disaster."

—Arnold Toynbee
The New York Times
March 19, 1971

The paramount energy question for America is
whether a nation which has created a voracious consumption monster will attempt to feed it, or try to
put it on a diet. How energy, a vital necessity affect-

ing the life of every person, could have been so completely taken for granted is in itself testimony to the remarkable success of the energy industries in developing supplies ahead of demands until the climax came in the 1970s.

In all the convenience and comfort of the 1970s there has been little awareness of the crucial contribution energy makes to the life and lifestyles of every American. There is little relationship between how a person lives and his knowledge that petroleum is a vital element not only in heating his home or fueling his automobile, but in fertilizing the food he eats and producing the medicines he takes.

Until recently energy was an always-handy, unobtrusive servant. It cooked and cleaned and lighted our homes. It entertained through television, radio and the movies and transported us to work and play. Even in the offices and in the factories, it did most of our physical and mental work through machines and computers. Most energy came by turning switches and dials, and relatively few individuals had any personal involvement with its problems.

Energy can no longer be taken for granted. The experience of turning down thermostats and waiting in long lines for gasoline dramatized the question of whether the United States could survive without increasing quantities of oil and whether meaningful substitutes were available.

Success has come easy to Americans, and we have developed a profound trust in the theology of scientific advancement through technology. This underlying attitude was trenchantly expressed by the chief executive of Standard Oil of California, who said, "People in our country are not used to running out of things."

For the United States, the Arab embargo provided the sobering shock that it is possible to run out of things. It was also a fortuitous preview of the Age of Scarcity which lies ahead for a broad array of important resources. Clearly, we have no real energy substitutes to replace petroleum—a fact overlooked during the past thirty years of abundant supplies.

Once we make a critical examination of oil and its precarious availability and increasing cost, it quickly becomes apparent that we cannot produce, nor can we afford to import, sufficient petroleum to meet the multiplying demands we can envision over the next decade.

The first reaction to the embargo was to find a scapegoat for the shortages. From consumer groups to congressional committees, from the oil corporations to independent truck drivers, there was a scurrying about looking for someone to blame. The name calling ranged widely from accusations about greedy oil corporations and irresponsible Arab leaders to denunciations of overzealous environmentalists and shortsighted governmental leaders. In varying degrees, each criticism had some validity. It was true, for example, that a multinational corporation, incorporated in the United States, pumping oil in Saudi Arabia, with refining operations in Holland and tankers under a Panamanian flag, and with assets larger than those of many sovereign nations, has conflicting loyalties and more than one master. But the problem is much bigger, and recriminations or a search for scapegoats will not produce a single kilowatt hour of energy.

If we believe some claims and estimates, we have enough coal for at least five hundred years; we can develop coal gasification techniques to keep all the gas fires burning; we can unlock oil shale to supply more oil than we have ever produced; and all those exciting, free, natural forms of energy—such as wind, sun, tides and geothermal heat from deep in the earth—will also keep U.S. energy consumption at very high levels.

What is important to realize now is that energy shortages will affect our lives significantly for at least the next two decades and will permanently alter the future. For Americans, the days of easy, inexpensive power are over, and all the golden-tomorrow futurologists, with their sunny optimism about the energy replacements that will produce undreamed-of power for our machines, had better take an objective look at the practical feasibility of their theories.

The Coal Contribution

How great a contribution can coal make as a replacement for petroleum? There are two possibilities. Coal can be put through a synthetic process that converts it into a gas which would be acceptable for consumers as a substitute for natural gas. There is also the prospect that coal can be "liquefied" and converted by a different process into a form of energy that could be a partial substitute for oil.

Since the Arab oil embargo, hyperbolic statements about America's abundance of coal have been repeated so often that they have become part of the new energy litany: the U.S. is a "coal-rich nation"; it "has enough coal to provide all the energy we need for four hundred or five hundred years." In a series of full-page newspaper advertisements in the spring of 1974, the American Electric Power Company, the nation's largest conglomerate collection of electric power, made this jingoistic proclamation: "If America is determined to get out from under the thumb of oil-rich nations, the shift to electricity generated by coal is not necessary, it is inevitable."

Conventional coal production can be increased to replace the inherently wasteful use of natural gas and oil for generating electricity. At the present time, coal supplies only 18 percent of our national energy needs, and almost two-thirds of it is used for the generation of electricity. The Nixon administration, which developed a sudden coal-bias when the Arab embargo hit, urged a 50% increase in coal production, from the 602 million tons mined in 1973 to 962 million tons by 1980. Considering the current debilitating labor, equipment and investment troubles in the coal industry, an expansion of this magnitude is an unrealistic target. Some increases in coal production will undoubtedly be achieved, but at this point it appears unlikely that synthetic coal can supplant dwindling supplies of petroleum. In 1974, there were no operating coal gasification or liquefication plants in this country.

Some coal spokesmen are making ambitious claims

that coal synthetics can be phased in as petroleum phases out. There are strong indications that these claims are wild exaggerations. Such optimism about large-scale conversion of Western coal sufficient to replace even a portion of the current consumption of natural gas or petroleum is unfounded and ignores serious issues of technology, economics, and environmental destruction. Although Hitler's Germany produced very modest amounts of oil from coal under the pressures of World War II, the technology of coal conversion has languished in the United States ever since pipelines began to bring Texas and Louisiana natural gas to the major markets in the Midwest and East about thirty years ago.

The largest supplies of suitable low-sulphur coal are found in the Rocky Mountain states. To produce any appreciable amount of high-grade gas or oil synthetically would require massive amounts of coal. As much as one ton of this coal would be used for every three barrels of oil produced, and the strip mining required to supply coal conversion plants large enough to substitute for any significant portion of our natural oil and gas needs would be staggering. Twice the output of the largest mines presently being worked would be needed, for example, to feed a synthetic oil plant producing 100,000 barrels of oil a day. Overall, the strip mining required to provide even a small portion of the current national oil needs would entail an earth-moving operation comparable to digging a Panama Canal every day.

The coal industry is already the primary despoiler of the environment of the United States, and the chewing up of Appalachia in previous strip mining would be insignificant compared to the size of the proposed large-scale mining of coal in several Western states. The iron laws of ecology also are a major obstacle to implementation of the technologies now contemplated. Synthetic coal plants would require huge amounts of water. Since much of the coal is situated in arid areas of the West, water may, indeed, be the restraint which limits the growth of coal synthetics.

The economics of any large-scale conversion in the West that is dependent upon strip-mining also cannot be overlooked. In addition to the tremendous capital investment in the equipment and machinery for stripping the coal, it is certain that state or federal environmental regulations will require costly restoration of the land surfaces exposed. Conversion plants themselves add enormous capital requirements. A single coal liquefication plant is estimated to cost nearly one-half billion dollars. The final balance sheet must also consider the energy demands of the coal conversion process itself. Strip mining uses energy. The proposed conversion plant itself will use large amounts of energy. In the long run, however, water shortages in the semi-arid regions of the West will in all likelihood be the vital factor in deciding whether coal conversion can make any significant contribution to our national energy budgets.

Oil Shale

Only the congenital optimists still believe that oil shale can replace more than a fraction of current U.S.

petroleum production within the next twenty years. Oil shale is marlstone rock that must be "cooked" to 900 degrees before liquefying. High-grade oil shale contains about 25 gallons of oil in each ton. Most of this high-grade shale is located in the arid Colorado and Green River basins; enough to yield at least 600 billion barrels of oil is estimated to exist under federal lands in Utah, Wyoming and Colorado. The infant oil shale industry, however, faces even more intimidating obstacles than the coal industry in the West.

Unlike petroleum production, the extraction of oil from the shale is primarily a mining operation. Until 1973, there were not even any serious offers to begin a mining and extraction operation on any of the public's oil shale lands. Now six leases are out on lands, which the federal government claims may produce a million barrels of oil a day in about ten years —about 10 percent of current petroleum production. Shale developers must mount a huge mining operation. Exxon's chairman, Ed Jamieson, has estimated that "We would have to develop a mining operation as big as the [present] coal industry just to provide 10 percent of current oil production."

The water demands for mining oil shale in sufficient quantities to support an oil shale industry of even 1 million barrels per day would be large by Western standards. Not only would water requirements be difficult to meet from existing sources, but the discharge water at the end of the process would be contaminated with minerals and would pose a threat to all downstream water users in this basin—including rich agricultural valleys in Arizona and California.

Compared with coal conversion, oil shale presents even greater waste problems. For every barrel of synthetic oil that might come from a coal conversion plant, nearly one-third of a ton of coal would be used. But for every barrel of synthetic oil that is produced from high-grade oil shale, almost a ton and a half of rock must be processed. After the oil is removed from the shale, more than a ton of wastes, increased 20 percent in volume, remain for disposal. If a group of plants were producing 1 million barrels of oil from shale each day, there would be approximately 833 tons of rock rubble every minute, or enough waste to fill a freight train of 700 hopper cars every hour.

Everything about the geography of the river basins where the oil shale is located says "go slow." The shale is situated in one of the most scenic, unspoiled, dry areas of the United States, and these considerations dictate wise stewardship. Since the public owns the great bulk of the shale which is beneath federal lands, a gradual development keyed to caution and conservation is the only policy which makes sense.

The Long-Term Outlook

The perspective in which each of the proposed long-term alternatives is evaluated is crucial. Under the "cheap energy" policy of the past, nearly all of the major decisions were made by energy companies that were influenced by the pulling and hauling of marketplace economics, by government policies that promoted the production of cheap energy, and by their own selfish desire to increase sales of the fuel they were producing. This unbridled system predictably produced contradictory results.

On the positive side, the coal and petroleum and electric power companies succeeded remarkably in achieving their singleminded goal of enlarging the nation's output of cheap energy. As long as our low-cost resources lasted, and the public was willing to stand aside and watch its own environmental assets be diminished and despoiled, the "cheap energy" policy was a success of sorts.

However, it is now clear that we paid a very high hidden price for our ready supplies of very cheap power. With the active encouragement of state and federal governments, the energy companies depleted our petroleum at a frightening rate: they fouled the air of our cities and turned whole valleys and regions like Appalachia into man-made wastelands; they developed a vested interest in the expansion of their own production, which caused them to promote the wasteful use of their product and to discourage more efficient, smaller-scale solutions to problems; they also acquired a bias for big engineering, which required huge amounts of investment capital. The federal government itself later compounded these errors by espousing nuclear power as the ultimate "solution" for all of our energy needs.

These industries still control the production and

distribution of energy in this country. If the various alternatives are to be seriously considered as possible replacements of traditional energy sources and systems, it is urgent that all the conflicting values be weighed so that balanced judgments and coordinated policies can eventually be formulated. One of the lessons of the past two decades is that we should not rely upon any one energy option for the future. The glamour of nuclear energy was so alluring that we pledged the bulk of our research-and-development dollars to this one uncertain source, virtually ignoring the charms and possibilities of other alternatives. We have now, hopefully, begun to realize in the tarnishing promise of nuclear energy that the balanced research and development of all energy options is probably the best investment for the future. The bulk of our remaining petroleum, coal and oil shale resources are in public ownership, and therefore are subject to bridled development. With our experience in instituting environmental controls, the necessary guidelines are now also available to assure that energy generation is accomplished without imparing urban environments or devastating the countryside.

Nuclear Power

Judging by the level of federal spending schedules for energy research and development through 1980, the government is still placing our big future bet on nuclear power. Of the $11.3 billion energy program, about half will be concentrated upon nuclear power.

The largest single item in this proposed outlay is the liquid metal fast breeder reactor.

Conventional nuclear power generation using the light-water and gas-cooled reactor is a short-lived, relatively inefficient and hazardous industry, plagued with demanding engineering problems. The first-generation nuclear reactors initially utilize less than 1 percent of the energy contained in natural uranium, and there are not enough uranium reserves at current prices to last for the lifetime of the nuclear plants now in existence. Additional lower-grade uranium reserves may be available, but only at costs which will increasingly make nuclear power less competitive.

Consequently, the big hopes of the nuclear power enthusiasts are pinned on the breeder reactor. The most attractive feature of the breeder, and the reason for its name, is that it makes more nuclear fuel than it consumes. In the process of splitting uranium atoms and producing heat for power generation, more atoms of fissionable material are produced than were on hand originally. While this increases the efficiency of the use of uranium ore, and supposedly solves the problem of long-term atomic fuel supply, it may not be economical to build breeders, and the operation of all kinds of reactors presents serious unresolved engineering and safety questions.

The fuel used in the breeder reactor will be man-made plutonium, the most lethal, long-lived poison ever introduced onto planet earth. Plutonium is also the explosive core of H-bombs. Because of the greater temperatures and pressures in a breeder reactor, and the use of liquid sodium as the heat transfer agent, the operation of this reactor presents engineering design problems which leave little margin for error, and may be insurmountable. A faulty valve or piece of equipment, or a breakdown in the human control systems, could trigger a catastrophic accident, which could release plutonium into the atmosphere. Estimated to be 100,000 times more poisonous than the venom of a cobra, and many thousand times more deadly than nerve gas, doses of plutonium dust breathed into the lungs can be lethal in a matter of minutes. Even in small amounts, tiny particles of plutonium dust will destroy the human lung in a matter of weeks. Worse yet, the millions of gallons of waste of breeder reactors will be lethal for tens of thousands of years, and present future generations for millennia to come with hideous problems of "perpetual care."

Optimistic scientists say these problems can be "handled"; the pessimists see the issue as an overriding moral problem for humanity, and argue that we should not continue to play God with the future of mankind in a situation where human misdeeds or miscalculations cannot be tolerated. One critic of the proposed AEC plan for building "mausoleums" for nuclear wastes, Washington attorney Anthony Z. Roisman, described the dilemma: "The Egyptians built the pyramids and placed an eternal curse on them. They were broken into before a hundred years. We have something that is cursed for more than a thousand years. Governments just haven't remained stable that long."

By increasing the amount of plutonium in circulation about the world, the wide proliferation of breeder reactors would also be an open invitation to desperate political terrorists to attempt to fashion crude nuclear weapons and hold the "great power" countries hostage to their demands. Those who are suggesting that we force unnumbered future generations to live with this cataclysmic risk may soon be perceived as the madmen of our era.

More than a billion dollars of federal money has already been spent on a breeder reactor and its alluring promise of perpetual cheap energy, and another $5.5 billion is allocated for this questionable project. The first U.S. experimental liquid metal fast breeder reactor is being built in Tennessee by the government and the nuclear industry, and is scheduled to be completed in the early 1980s. The final decision on this project will be a fateful one of human ethics.

Nuclear fission releases energy through the splitting of the atomic nucleus and is the process which powered the first atomic bomb. The most powerful thermonuclear device, the hydrogen bomb, duplicates the fusion process of the sun and the stars. Here, the nuclei of two atoms of deuterium (so-called "heavy hydrogen") are fused together to make one atom of helium. In this reaction, an incredible amount of energy is released. Since the mid-1950s, scientists have been trying to harness the reaction of the hydrogen bomb under controlled conditions in a laboratory. The difficulties of producing a contained, sustained fusion of heavy hydrogen atoms and capturing the released energy are enormous. Temperatures of over

100 million degrees are needed to initiate a fusion reaction, which must then be maintained under control long enough and continuously enough to produce an energy surplus.

While fusion reactors would not be without some environmental risks, the theoretical advantages of nuclear fusion over nuclear fission—particularly the fast breeder—are significant. First of all, the heavy hydrogen fuel for fusion reactors would be readily obtained from the oceans. Unlike fission reactors, a fusion reactor would contain no materials suitable for diversion to clandestine bombs. In addition, the radioactivity hazards of either reactor malfunctions or accidents would be many thousand times smaller with fusion than with an equivalent breeder reactor. Not only would the fusion reaction be fundamentally easier to shut down should a mishap occur, the long-lived radioative wastes which plague the present-generation fission reactors, and which will be multiplied by the breeder, are subject to greater design and manufacture control in a possible fusion reactor. The fusion reactor also has the potential for the direct conversion of electricity, a much more efficient process than passing through normal generation of electricity where wasted heat becomes an important environmental problem.

For all the potential advantages of nuclear fusion, it is still a technological longshot. Efforts are under way in several countries, including the United States and Russia, to use magnetic forces and concentrated laser beams to initiate and control the fusion process in a laboratory. However, at present there is no technique to control and contain these awesome "fires." Until this first major breakthrough is achieved in the laboratory, however, nuclear fusion will not figure in our long-range plans for alternative sources of energy. And at the moment, the scientific, engineering and economic questions which now enshroud the potential of nuclear fusion in doubt are sure to remain unanswered, while the bulk of the nuclear research efforts are concentrated on putting the breeder reactor into operation.

Coal and Shale and the "In Situ" Process

Beyond the near future and the conventional exploitation of coal and oil shale deposits, there is an unperfected process for extracting the energy from these fossil fuels which deserves analysis. This process involves cooking coal or shale underground "in place" without having to mine it. Various methods are proposed for this type of recovery, but they all basically involve fracturing large quantities of the mineral underground so that it is permeable and then igniting it. In theory, with oil shale, the heated gases would vaporize the oil to be condensed and captured above ground; with coal, the introduction of steam and oxygen would be used to gasify the fuel in its underground seams.

If an acceptable process can be evolved, obviously it would have many advantages. Strip mining impacts could be decreased or largely eliminated, and the capital investments required could be substantially reduced.

Another advantage cited for "in situ" is that this process would probably make much smaller demands on other resources, particularly water. Nevertheless, there is one particular consideration which must be kept in the forefront as various "in place" plans are evaluated. Any method which either uses up inordinate amounts of coal or shale as the "process" fuel to "fire" the extraction process itself, or which leaves enormous quantities of coal or shale in the ground unexploited (by only recovering a fraction of the total resource available) would be profligate and rob future generations of resources they might desperately need. Coal and oil shale will obviously be crucial "transition fuels" until permanent renewable sources are developed. They should be used with prudence until reliable alternatives are achieved.

Hydrogen

If hydrogen could be be developed as a vehicle for the transportation of energy, it would have some of the convenience and versatility of natural gas. It would probably be synthesized from water by electrolysis or processed biologically from organic matter. It will take huge amounts of energy to produce major quantities of hydrogen, however, and any large-scale effort will probably involve big floating nuclear power stations in the oceans. The energy stored in hydrogen would be distributed via pipelines, like natural gas, or as a liquid at low temperatures. While hydrogen is somewhat more explosive than natural gas, it is clean and nonpolluting and can be used like natural gas, or in individual applications at the site of direct use.

The cost of the electricity required to "split" water is the main obstacle today to the development of hydrogen as a major new type of fuel. Currently it would cost ten times more to manufacture hydrogen than the wellhead price of natural gas.

Geothermal Energy

The exploitation of the heat trapped in the interior of the earth to produce usable forms of energy has been underway for decades. Up until now, however, the harnessing of the earth's heat has only occurred at sites where there are natural outcroppings of hot water or steam. Geothermal steam has been used in Iceland for space heating for years, and now heats nearly the entire capital city of Reykjavik, including swimming pools and nearby greenhouses. The earliest commercial utilization of geothermal energy took place in Italy in 1904 when dry steam was used to power an electric generating plant that is still operating today. In the United States, the Pacific Gas and Electric Company has been using dry steam from the geothermal fields north of San Francisco, known as The Geysers, to generate electric power since 1960 at costs lower than comparable nuclear or fossil fuel plants. Additional generating units are planned for The Geysers which will raise the capacity from 396 megawatts to nearly three times that amount, or approximately enough power output to satisfy the electricity demands of a city the size of San Francisco. So far, The Geysers is the only venture in the United States to commercially harness geothermal energy.

While some eighty countries in the world have geological conditions which offer the potential for geothermal operations, only eight countries presently use these underground resources and now generate about the same amount of electric power that is ultimately projected for The Geysers. The total world geothermal-electric generating capacity of about 1000 megawatts is only the size of a conventional large fossil fuel power plant. Because the contribution of geothermal sources will always be limited by geology to those areas where hot springs or geysers bring the heat of the earth close to the surface, this supply of energy will never be anything more than supplementary and regional.

Experimental efforts are now underway in Montana to try to expand the potential for geothermal energy by probing much deeper into the earth's interior to reach hot or molten rock. One proposed method is to apply advanced petroleum technology and, after preliminary drilling, inject water under high pressure down into the bowels of the earth into dry hot rock formations. After these deep water injections hydraulically fracture the hot rock, the heated water would be returned to the surface to directly drive the turbine of an electric power generator or indirectly transfer heat to a secondary fluid which would circulate through the turbines. All these deep underground efforts, however, are still strictly experimental efforts involving expensive drilling techniques. In addition, at the underground levels that must be reached, substances are encountered which are highly corrosive and which present sophisticated mechanical problems in controlling and disposing of these dissolved mineral salts and noxious gasses. Hot or molten rock under the crust of the earth will undoubtedly be much more difficult to successfully and economically harness than steam or hot water near the surface. It is unlikely, therefore, that geothermal energy will ever do more than make a modest contribution to energy supplies in particular regions of the world.

Oceanic Energy Potential

Capturing the energy potential of other natural phenomena—such as the tides, the currents of the oceans, and the temperature differences of various layers of tropical waters—offers as limited promise as does the use of geothermal sources in selected portions of the world. So far, most efforts in the oceans have concentrated on damming estuaries and bays which are intermittently filled and emptied by the twice-daily tides, using this flow of water to move turbines and generate electric power. Such dams and turbine installations are massive and expensive investments. The tides will not provide a steady supply of power without additional advancements which even the flow of tidal water or store energy between the tidal peaks.

Only two installations in the world presently harness the ocean energy of the tides and generate electricity. In 1966, France began capturing tidal power on the coast of Brittany with a 240-megawatt plant. Two years later, the Russians began operating a small 400-kilowatt experimental plant that uses the rising and falling tides of the Barents Sea. Other suitable locations exist throughout the world where tides are sufficiently large to warrant installation of major tidal-electric power plants. Canada has the largest tidal fluctuation in the world—55 feet—in the areas along the Bay of Fundy. If this region, and all other particularly well-suited locations in the world, were exploited for their tidal energy, however, the additional electricity that could be generated is estimated to be as low as 13,000 megawatts—the equivalent of thirteen conventional large fossil fuel power plants.

Other proposals for taking advantage of renewable forms of ocean energy supplied by the sun and the gravitational pull of the sun and the moon are still very experimental and exist largely in theory. Suggestions have been made to anchor vast numbers of low-revolution turbines in tropical waters and the Atlantic Gulf Stream to translate ocean currents and temperature variations into electricity. Whether these turbines are to be run by the surface currents of the Gulf Stream, which may exceed 5 miles per hour, or whether they take advantage of the variations in temperature between surface and lower layers of tropical waters to circulate a secondary liquid such as ammonia, awesome technical problems and uncertain environmental issues challenge the idea that any significant amount of power can ever be obtained outside the laboratory. Hardware which can remain anchored in the ocean, resist the corrosion of sea water, and operate sealed generating units that circulate a low-boiling fluid do not exist. If any amount of power is ever produced, there are unanswered problems of storage and transmission to desired mainland areas. A more troublesome question which must be thoroughly investigated involves the possible impact which any tampering with the energy of the Atlantic Gulf Stream might have on the climate of northern Europe. Until such elemental and practical engineering and environmental issues are further explored, such methods to tap ocean energy are still flights of fancy.

Solar and Wind Energy

Two highly promising natural renewable sources of energy—solar and wind power—can be implemented on a large scale in ten or fifteen years if we would only accord them the priority they deserve. The ancients had the right instinct in worshippng the sun; it is the primal source of life. With all of man's modern artificial-energy generating activities, he still only produces a daily amount of energy equivalent to about 1 percent of the radiant energy which arrives each twenty-four hours from the sun. And 96 percent of the energy of the United States today is provided by fossil fuels—oil, natural gas and coal—which are actually stored forms of solar energy.

There is a natural linkage between solar and wind energy. Wind currents are formed by sun power and there is a growing awareness among scientists that these two sources will probably become a complementary energy team. Small-scale sun and wind power sources are particularly promising, for, as the search for long-term energy alternatives deepens, the highest priority must be given to solutions that are inexpensive and nonpolluting, that work *with* nature, and that offer energy dividends for everyone, and not just the highly industrialized nations.

In essence, there are two quite different kinds of solar energy applications under consideration. The first would use big technology to power industrial furnaces or generate electric power which could be fed into conventional electric grid systems for distribution along normal utility transmission lines. Such big dreams of solar application envision "solar ranching" installations in desert areas, giant solar furnaces using parabolic mirrors, or huge satellites in outer space beaming power to earth via microwaves. Research should be started on these big-technology alternatives, but economic and environmental constraints make it unlikely that any meaningful contribution will come from them until well into the twenty-first century.

On the other hand, if we give a big push to small-scale solar-wind installations, they might provide most of the energy needs for our homes and commercial buildings, say, twenty years from now. Given the necessary encouragement, solar-wind combinations could supply a significant segment of our energy needs this century. The basic technologies are already available and do not depend upon massive engineering efforts of hook-ups with large utilities. Sophisticated new windmills, solar panels, and batteries can be mass produced if the government provides the initial subsidies and policies which are needed to achieve a takeoff in this area.

These kinds of solar energy are renewable indefinitely, have a zero impact upon the environment, entail relatively modest investments of capital by the owners of homes and other buildings, require minimal energy to operate for space heating and cooling, and can be exploited by using small, easily maintained technologies within the reach of all nations.

A joint panel of the National Aeronautics and Space Administration and the National Science Foundation estimated recently that within ten years small-scale solar energy could save $180 million in fuel costs and supply more than one-third of the space heating and cooling in the country, and about one-fifth of the electricity.

The Conversion of "Wastes"

Until now we have overlooked the energy values in our own "wastes." Garbage, sewage, animal wastes

and decaying plants have substantial value as recyclable future fuels.

The most obvious immediate method of capturing
the energy in urban refuse is to imitate existing
European installations and burn trash and garbage
to generate electricity and produce steam for home
heating. Urban refuse and the organic wastes of animals feedlots can also be converted into oil and gas
by pyrolysis, a high-temperature distillation process in
the absence of air.

Perhaps an even more versatile and promising
method of converting all of society's organic wastes—
sewage, animal and agricultural wastes, urban refuse
and garbage—is offered by the airless bacterial decomposition of these residues into methane gas or
methanol. Bacterial fermentation of the organic
matter in an air-tight vessel or digestor can produce
significant and useful quantities of fuel (as methane)
in a variety of sizes of application from the individual
home to the large refuse dump or livestock feedlot.
The fermentation of organic wastes to produce
methane gas or methanol alcohol requires no startling scientific discoveries. It is merely imitating
nature and promoting rapid decay. Natural gas is
nothing more than the ancient end result of the
millennial decomposition of plants.

The General Prospect

All replacement energy is "paper energy" until
processes have been perfected or plants capable of

large-scale production are built. But in a nation that has always had more than it ever needed, optimism dies hard. The technology to develop these alternate sources has been too long neglected and disastrously underfinanced, mainly because oil was so cheap and plentiful that the experts felt there was no need to bother with what they called "exotic" energy sources.

During the early stages of the Arab oil embargo, President Nixon, in a national television address, introduced the idea of "Project Independence" as the answer to the U.S. energy crisis. He said:

> Let us set as our national goal, in the spirit of Apollo, with the determination of the Manhattan Project, that by the end of this decade we will have developed the potential to meet our energy needs without depending on any foreign energy sources. Let us pledge that by 1980, under Project Independence, we shall be able to meet America's energy needs from America's own energy resources.

Unfortunately, that announcement was an exercise in energy sloganeering. It will take much more than the politicians' cliché of calling for a Manhattan Project or an Apollo Project to solve the enormous energy problems of the next three decades.

The comparison of such an effort to obtain self-sufficiency by 1980 to the space or atomic bomb project is highly inappropriate and very misleading. Both the Manhattan Project and the Apollo program had very narrowly defined goals and were essentially totally financed and controlled by the federal government with the assistance of private contractors.

Economic interactions with other sectors of the economy were minor, and both projects were not in competition with private enterprise. The production and consumption of energy, however, is a complex mix which accounts for a significant portion of our economic activity and touches every part of our society.

To achieve the goal of Project Independence would mean coming up with an estimated energy equivalent of 9 million barrels of additional oil every day by the end of the decade. As the administration's own energy experts and officials have stated, there are no production wonder machines on the shelf ready to be plugged into the national energy system. And any thoroughgoing effort to achieve such a goal by 1980 would depend upon the reckless exploitation of our remaining oil and gas reserves, and the massive stripping of coal—measures that would involve tremendous environmental damage and the too rapid depletion of the remaining petroleum resources.

The one dominating fact that bears constant repetition is there are no substitutes in sight for oil and gas, the two sources that comprise over three-quarters of the U.S. energy supply. It will not be easy to develop any of the so-called alternate sources to replace even part of the current petroleum-dominated energy system, nor will extravagant predictions about hard-to-develop resources help.

What is now necessary is a factual approach that will develop realistic national policies based on verifiable facts and feasible technology. Americans have always taken pride in their pragmatism. Now that pragmatism should work to help us surrender the energy illusions and unfounded technological expectations that still distort our outlook.

Unless a very high priority is given to an extensive research and development program, "alternative energy" sources will turn out to be the new hocus-pocus slogan of the technological optimists.

All of the alternatives face enormous problems. Expectations for a future nonpetroleum-dominated, mixed-energy society must be tempered by the realization that it will take fifteen to twenty years to significantly alter the vast, complex energy systems that now exist. In addition to the strictly technological questions, there are also formidable interrelated economic, environmental and social obstacles.

The perplexing irony of the alternate-energy transition is that nearly every alternative will end up using substantial oil to replace oil, making the development of some alternative sources that much more difficult and expensive. Whether one considers the fuel necessary for mining and refining, or fuel for transportation and the distribution of the new sources, some petroleum will be required for the development of alternate energy sources.

An important judgment to be made in assessing each energy alternative is not only its cost in dollars, but also the amount of energy consumed to produce energy. In some cases all the related known and hidden costs to produce a unit of energy—economic, environmental, transportation, production and distribution—may be too high to be practical.

From now on the true costs of each alternative must be considered. These choices must be evaluated by using the "net energy" concept which puts ecology and economics in common focus for the first time. Such a concept weighs the financial assistance—government subsidies, lifetime capital costs—as well as the environmental demands and damages which must be invested in any particular energy system in order to produce a unit of power.

The present experience has no precedent in the nation's energy history. Earlier transitions from one dominant fuel to another, such as the shift from wood to coal, occurred because a superior fuel with greater efficiency and versatility emerged and elbowed inferior fuel aside. This time the versatile fossil fuels are depleting, with no real replacement sources ready.

For three decades, oil and gas have dominated the U.S. energy market. The production and use of petroleum products has also largely determined the capital investment and research and development efforts of private industry. During the same period the federal government concentrated practically all of its subsidies on the "nuclear option." This was shortsighted because research efforts into other alternate sources were largely ignored.

In 1963, more than 90 percent of the $330 million the federal government spent on energy research went to nuclear power. Private industry during that same year ventured more than half of its $614 million on oil and gas research. In 1974, the two patterns of research spending had not changed significantly. Industry was still allocating more than 70 percent of its

$1 billion research efforts to oil and gas. Although the federal government had stepped up its coal research effort, three-quarters of the $755 million invested in energy in 1974 went for nuclear development.

The enormous ongoing financial commitments involved in altering the nation's energy supplies in the future and providing a varied energy mix further complicate the development of viable alternatives. Ten percent of the nation's economic activity is currently involved in producing, distributing and consuming energy. With a Gross National Product of about $1.3 trillion, powerful economic and industrial cross currents will be set in motion if efforts are made to change the mix of the $125-billion-a-year market.

After examining all the alternatives, it is apparent that energy "lead times" are very long and the opportunity to reshape what happens in the next decade has already been largely foreclosed. The near-term outlook is bleak. It is depressing that there are still industrial and political voices boasting about "energy independence by 1980" and "America has energy to burn." These arguments are founded on a belief that somehow we can: achieve major increases in U.S. petroleum production by a big increase in offshore leasing or by a major effort to increase the amount of oil recovered from existing oil fields by what are called "secondary" and "tertiary" methods; rely on increased supplies of coal and the gasification of coal on a scale large enough to allow it to replace much of our dwindling natural gas reserves; produce enough oil from oil shale to significantly augment total U.S. output of petroleum.

Most oil wells in the United States only recover about 30 percent of the oil in the ground. The primary recovery is usually about 20 percent and is brought up by natural water and gas pressure. When "primary" recovery fails, "secondary" recovery rates of an additional 10 to 20 percent can be achieved by introducing high-pressure water into the field to artificially build back the underground pressure.

Further recovery is possible after flooding has been utilized by using "tertiary" methods, or so-called "exotics." These "exotics" involve introducing heat or solvents such as alcohol into the field to increase the flow and add perhaps another 10 percent to the total rate of recovery. The tertiary methods, however, are not perfected and are expensive.

As for further increases by more rigorous secondary recovery processes, big jumps in onshore expansion of domestic oil production are not immediately feasible without endangering the possible total recovery over the life of the wells. With careful regulation of the rate at which oil is extracted from a well or, more precisely, from an entire field, the total recovery of oil can be greatly increased. If rapid exploitation of a field occurs and the valves are turned wide open for a quick payoff, in most cases a much smaller percentage of the petroleum can be ultimately recovered.

It will also be important to realize that some of the proposals for optional forms of energy place an inordinate burden on the electric power industry—one of the least efficient users of the primary forms of energy. For every unit of energy the consumer uses, the power utilities burn up three units in generating and transmitting the electricity. The electric power industry should eventually become the workhorse for the industrial sector and provide the clean energy we need for such amenities as electric trains and trolleys. As renewable sources such as solar and wind power are perfected for on-site total energy systems for homes, commercial buildings and cluster housing, electric roles will change.

More versatile, flexible systems that fit the needs—and resources—of different geographic regions must be developed. Simplistic answers such as the arrogant pratings of the American Electric Power Company that "the most sensible way to help solve the energy shortage is to generate more electricity" through the burning of coal are not helpful. There is nothing sensible in responding to the energy shortages by making ill-considered long-term commitments to one form of energy which may foreclose better choices a few years from now.

Learning from the energy mistakes of the past thirty years and looking at future requirements through the turn of the century, we clearly must not invest the bulk of our research efforts and money in a single "cure-all" option. If we had, for example, only spent a portion of the huge amounts invested in subsidizing the nuclear energy industry for basic research, development and demonstration of such alternatives as wind, solar heating and cooling, methanol, geothermal and the utilization of our wastes, the energy impasse in 1974 would have been much less severe. Through the singular dependence upon only one resource, petroleum, and the single-minded "bet" on one solution for the future, irreplaceable lead time was lost.

The primary task now is to develop a frugal national lifestyle that conserves and husbands oil supplies to prolong the petroleum age as long as possible. This generation will be anathema to its children and grandchildren if it plunders its continental shelves—or overpumps its existing wells—on the assumption that the present is only responsible for the present, while the future is the future's problem.

chapter five

NEW ATTITUDES AND LEANER LIFESTYLES

"The trouble with our time is that the future is not what it used to be."

—Paul Valéry

The only reasonable course for the United States is to admit that it is in trouble and begin a transition to a lifestyle and an economy which emphasize thrift and efficiency. Significant changes cannot be avoided. We can no longer sit comfortably in our horseless chariots, dazzled by the promises of prosperity and technology run amuck.

Clearly the future is not what it used to be. Within a few years, a chronic shortage of energy will force a complete readjustment of the way the country produces, consumes and lives. That transition can be a gradual one of wise adjustments, or it can take the form of wrenching dislocations that will disrupt the economy and our lives.

If the country is prudent, it will seize the initiative and convert these ineluctable forces into an opportunity for creative change. This challenge can shatter a system that is too rigid to adapt, or it can permanently alter our transportation system, our industrial economy, our architecture, the design of our cities and the personal lives of each individual.

The energy crisis has bewildered Americans. It has revealed a vulnerability in the largest industrial firms —the auto and energy companies. It has revealed the failure of government to comprehend the dangers of collisions between finite resources and the voracious consumption habits of an affluent society.

The American public, unaccustomed to making sacrifices, needs leaders who will point out that Americans can no longer live their lives as though they were the only inhabitants of this planet. Without leaders who advocate a less wasteful lifestyle, the dream of the energy alchemists that scientific and diplomatic wizardry can keep the good old American growth machine rolling along has been perpetuated.

With the removal of the Middle East oil embargo in the spring of 1974, the administration rushed to announce that the energy crisis was over, Congress searched for energy devils to exorcise for their role in restricting oil supplies while garnering obscene profits, and industry tried to move back into production as usual. Instead of thoughtful proposals for conservation and efficiency, the emphasis has been on keeping the fuel pipelines flowing. Some electric power companies embarked on major national newspaper advertising campaigns to announce that the ultimate answer to the problem was the greater use of electricity generated from coal. In their view, this could only be accomplished by exploiting the coal under public lands in the West and by reducing air pollution standards that limit sulfur emissions from power plants. Some domestic oil producers rushed to pump remaining United States oil supplies faster and argued for accelerated development of the Outer Continental Shelf. Other business interests seized the opportunity to push for the removal of any barriers, environmental or otherwise, which inhibit the fastest possible growth of power production.

Detroit also announced its own business-as-usual plans. All of a sudden, an incredulous nation was informed of the automakers' serious, long-term commitment to the production of gas-thrifty automobiles. Only Detroit's "small" cars are not really small, and most of the engines are still very inefficient. In its best cotton-candy puffery, the automakers were once again investing in advertising as opposed to performance. They also saw a chance to divert attention from the fuel wasted by their heavy, gadget-filled, air-conditioned, automatic transmission cars by blaming their woes on air pollution controls. Their aim was not to provide smaller, more energy-conserving automobiles, but to sell their "family size" cars at Cadillac prices with all the options. It was still the same old message: Plan for the best and the biggest and expect nothing less.

Our energy predicament dictates that the U.S. cannot continue to increase its rate of consumption. It will be a remarkable achievement if the oil companies keep U.S. petroleum production anywhere near current levels in the years ahead, and any further increases in foreign imports will strain the economy and further unbalance the nation's balance of payments. The growing pressures to speed up petroleum production, nuclear power generation, coal production and any other forms of energy resource exploitation will only ensure that our generation will be remembered for its irrationality.

More than sixty-five years ago, the great conservationist president, Theodore Roosevelt, warned against such greedy, shortsighted use of resources:

> To avoid that slight shortage at the moment, there are certain people so foolish that they will incur absolute shortage in the future, and they are willing to stop all attempts to conserve the forests, because of course by wastefully using them at the moment we can for a year or two provide against any lack of wood. This is like providing for the farmer's family to live sumptuously on the flesh of the milk cow. Any farmer can live pretty well for a year if he is content not to live at all the year after.

U.S. consumption habits, based on convenience, throwaway and waste, must be replaced by an ethic that requires maximum use of everything and preserves fundamental human values. Most importantly, Americans must understand that true energy independence is not to be found in oil shale or in the continental shelves or in nuclear energy. Rather, it lies in greater individual self-sufficiency and a frugal use of present resources.

The changes needed will affect everyone and will be as basic as the way Americans live, eat, move about and work. A sensible, leaner lifestyle will eliminate waste by accepting the responsibility that this society has no right to squander the resources of future generations. The decisions made by the United States in dealing with the energy shortage will have repercussions throughout the world.

In sum, the broad changes (some of which will be explained in greater detail in succeeding chapters) must include not only tangible categories like transportation, but abstract concepts like education and self-sufficiency.

Transportation

To begin with, vast structural changes must be made in our transportation system. Transportation is one of the great organizing factors in American social and economic life. Present shortages are a warning that the extravagant automobile culture must shrink. We can get by with millions of cars for another decade or so only if they are small ones. If the suffocation of our cities and the collapse of suburban America are to be prevented, first-rate systems of mass transit must be built. If efficient intercity transportation is necessary, the railroad must have a renaissance. If there is to be life-giving movement in our cities, they must be equipped with walkways and bikeways.

Such changes can ease the shortages, save thousands of lives, reduce air pollution (resulting in health benefits and economic savings) and provide

Spillovers

innumerable bonuses for individuals and communities. With fewer automobiles and more efficient, inexpensive public transportation, and a curb on unnecessary driving, there will be less traffic congestion, and the air will be healthier and the streets safer.

Economically, savings accumulated by building fewer streets and expressways can be invested in mass transportation. There will also be less money spent on medical bills; auto injuries and the indirect health problems caused by air pollution, to which the automobile is a prime contributor, will be considerably reduced.

Where and How We Live

The end of urban sprawl and the revitalization of the older cities, two developments implicit in the dethronement of the auto, will make significant contributions to American life. The end of sprawl signals the end of escapism—the end of a flight from community problems and social responsibility and a reaffirmation of the importance of neighborhoods. Less mobility should mean less rootless wandering and a resurgence of community spirit. People who sink roots in a neighborhood that is vibrantly alive and contains pleasant amenities, necessary services and recreational facilities do not easily surrender to destructive forces such as real estate block-busting or urban renewal and expressways.

The older cities, where population density and

proximity of services allow the more efficient use of energy, offer excellent opportunities for renovation of dilapidated, worn-out neighborhoods. Similar results can also be achieved in the suburbs and future planned communities if a new approach to urban design is implemented—one that will put people first in order to create intimate environments which resemble the neighborhood arrangements exemplified in areas of some older U.S. cities. The buildings in which we live and work must also be designed according to the neighborhood concept; they must be alive with varied activities and use the best ideas for energy use and conservation.

Land Use and Slow Growth

Just as the burgeoning growth of the past thirty years is becoming illogical and expensive gasoline is making travel by private car uneconomical, new land use policies are imperative and future development will require a new kind of planning.

Even before the energy squeeze, there was an increasing resistance across the nation to the old policies of piecemeal growth and a questioning of the traditional chant, "growth is good; growth is inevitable." In some of the faster growing areas of the nation new attitudes are taking hold, ranging from demands for no-growth to an insistence on total environment planning.

From Palo Alto, California, to Eastport, Maine, citizens are opposing ill-planned expansion or development projects which heedlessly sacrifice values esteemed by local communities. Environmental protection is supplanting "growth for growth's sake" as the central concept of U.S. progress.

In all parts of the country, new forces and values are asserting themselves. For example, in St. Petersburg, Florida, and in Boulder, Colorado, governmental action has been taken to limit the extent of future growth. Both cities feel they have grown too fast and must slow or halt the pace of recent decades. In Oregon, the governor greets tourists who visit his state with the admonition, "Enjoy your stay, but for heaven's sake don't come here to live."

Two years ago in Colorado, voters rejected using state funds for the 1976 Winter Olympics; they thus scored a unique victory over powerful commercial interests, which based their case on the businessman's shibboleth that an economic bonanza would enrich the state. The electorate feared the event and its publicity would have a disastrous affect on their environment. They told the Olympics' promoters to take their project somewhere else.

In Florida, Governor Reuben Askew has strongly supported controlled growth as a new state policy. And Fairfax County, Virginia, one of the fastest growing areas in the country and a suburb of Washington, D.C., has attempted to confine further residential and commercial development because the county is unable to keep up with the demand for public services.

Industry

Never will go-lean policies have more beneficent results for the economy and the environment than when U.S. industry changes its basic practices and uses its allotted energy with efficiency. Industrial production uses more than 40 percent of the total energy consumed in this country. When shortages force industry to foreswear its spendthrift commitment to planned obsolescence and return to the manufacturing of long-lived goods and products, there will not only be substantial savings of energy, but large savings of precious raw materials as well. Once industry improves the efficiency of its production and distribution systems and accepts recycling of materials and energy as a new way of life, the whole nation will gain.

Men and Machines

There is also a human side to such an industrial reformation. There are early indications that higher energy costs will reduce the proliferating mechanization and automation of industry which has transformed much modern factory production into a tedious pushing of buttons and a tending of dials. If energy costs make automation an extravagant alternative, the opportunity to gain a more meaningful role in the manufacturing process might well be a major gain for U.S. workers. In some cases, less automation may result in higher prices for products—but then increased fuel costs for automation will also raise prices.

The most significant benefit will accrue to workers who have seen labor-saving machines and automated systems dehumanize their employment. Designed to improve productive capacity, automation makes work so monotonous that dramatically improved wages and benefits—which ostensibly allow the average employee to live the "good life"—are not enough to overcome the deep dissatisfaction which many Americans feel toward their jobs. As a result, quality in production has declined and slow-downs and absenteeism in the factories have increased. Labor disputes, especially in the auto industry, have not been attacks on labor-saving, high production, automated machinery in an effort to preserve jobs, as was historically the case; rather, they have been desperate attempts to preserve sane working conditions.

One of the angriest examples of this disenchantment occurred at a Lordstown, Ohio, General Motors assembly plant for the Vega automobile, where high wages and substantial fringe benefits were not sufficient to allay deep discontent among assembly line employees. As one twenty-year-old worker told Stanley Aronowitz, author of *False Promises,*

> Every day I come out of there I feel ripped off. I'm gettin' the shit kicked out of me and I'm helpless to stop it. A good day's work is being tired but not exhausted. Out there all I feel is glad when it's over. I don't even feel useful now. They could replace me; I

> don't even feel necessary. . . . They could always find
> somebody stupider than me to do the job.

As some assembly line workers see it, over-automation means a loss of identity or pride in craftsmanship in a struggle to keep up with ever-faster assembly lines, where the worker has one small repetitive task that he barely has time to complete before the next unit arrives at his station. In such energy-intensive, high-pressure systems, the only thing that matters is the number of production units completed every hour. It is difficult for a worker to explain what he does to his children, or anyone else, when his work is often a minor mechanical part of the finished product.

European manufacturing plants, principally Volvo's new assembly line in Kalmar, Sweden, and the new International Business Machine assembly plant in Amsterdam, have instituted systems to give the workers on the line more responsibility and control over the whole manufacturing process.

At the Volvo plant, workers have production goals and can work toward them at their own pace. The workers are divided into teams of about fifteen men and women, and each team is responsible for one production phase—for example, the installation of the electrical system or the interior upholstery.

At I.B.M., Amsterdam, teams of about twenty persons each produce a complete and recognizable model. Under the old assembly line process, workers complained they were robots, and production quality fell off. Employee disenchantment was so high that 12 percent of man-hours were spent in overtime for the repair of defective machines coming off the line. Thirty percent of the work force left their jobs each year, and absenteeism was a serious problem.

Since the new mini-assembly lines were installed at I.B.M. in 1971, production has risen, quality has improved and overtime has been reduced. Absenteeism and personnel turnover have also dropped. The new Volvo line hasn't existed long enough for a significant analysis, but company officials are pleased with initial results.

In making the production process less wasteful of power, manufacturers have an opportunity to redesign and experiment with methods that will permit the individual employee to participate more in that process and to identify more with the finished product. His work thus becomes a meaningful part of his life.

Education

Two important facets of the leaner, simpler lifestyle are individual self-sufficiency and employment opportunities that emphasize craftsmanship rather than mechanized, assembly line manufacturing. In a society that offers abundant leisure time to many of its members, the modern concept of a career education—the all-embracing idea of preparing students for useful jobs—should give way to the view that education is a key to the rewarding use of one's leisure time. Once Americans understand that leisure is vitally important, there will be no stigma attached ("What a waste of a good education!") to a person with an advanced academic degree who chooses to work as a cab driver or butcher or shoe repairman. Education won't exist solely to help him find a role in the economy, but rather to enrich his private life and his role as a citizen.

With the revival of the cities as places to live, there will be more determination to elevate the standards of the urban schools to the level of the suburban schools, and there will be an effort to see that they get the financial support necessary to achieve high academic standards. School buildings will then become community centers, available during non-school hours as meeting places; recreational areas; and sites for neighborhood parties, governmental political forums, and adult and continuing education programs.

Values and Attitudes

Education has been the foundation of American society. The cementing force has been science and technology, using easily obtained resources and directing the forces of production and consumption. Because science and technology were successful on a grand scale, it was the common belief that every new idea that worked was also necessary. Once an idea was developed, it was mass produced and distributed nationwide. As a result, many established institutions were changed: the family farmer gave way to the agricultural business corporation; the corner grocer was eliminated by the national food chain; the small businessman became a corporation; and many corporations grew into greedy, dangerous conglomerates and multinationals. Government and other public institutions became indispensable partners through policies, programs, subsidies, tax benefits and access to public resources.

But along with all the complex technology and all the accompanying benefits and comforts came a grasping, insatiable mentality that measured success in country club memberships, well-kept lawns, the size of a car one owned. Prestige was even based on such irrelevant criteria as the size of one's office, the relative assets of a corporation, and the size of the city in which one lived. It was a system where status was judged by superficial values and where human worth had little meaning.

The wasteful use of energy often created a selfish and self-indulgent desire for additional empty materialistic goods and gadgets. Yet for every material indulgence, there have been irreplaceable losses that cannot be measured by monetary values. Another price was paid in the deterioration of diversity, continuity, community, shared goals, responsibility and individual sufficiency and pride. It is these resources that sustain the individual, the family, the community and in turn the entire society.

The options before the American people are not simply growth and stagnation. If we exercise restraint and learn to live comfortably within our means, we can find ample opportunities for a full and vital life of variety, diversity, choice and quality.

It is perhaps an all-but-forgotten heritage, but deep within the American character, numbed and stultified, is a conservative frugality that valued thrift and abhorred waste. Such values will again come to the forefront as the Age of Scarcity forces us to change our ways.

The recent period of superabundance is a historical aberration. It has made possible the bureaucratization of society, and has spawned national attitudes of sloth and a self-centered "I've-got-mine-Jack" approach to community needs and the rights of fellow citizens.

A leaner lifestyle, concerned about the energy it spends, emphasizes simple things, not impersonal, complex systems. Solar energy, for instance, is one of those simple, individualistic ways to keep warm and run machinery. But all this time it has been generally ignored. As the writer E. B. White wistfully observed: "The sun. Solar heat should be captured and used. A cat dozing in the sunny doorway of a barn knows all about it. Why can't man learn?" Man can't seem to learn because he has come to believe machines will do everything for him and somehow life will always be better.

What will a leaner lifestyle be like and why will it be better than the way Americans live now? In an unplanned, unorganized fashion, without governmental or social sanction, the younger generation has already begun questioning prevailing values and consumption habits. There has been considerable writing and discussion about the "new youth movement" in recent years, and there has been some misguided imitation of the "youth culture" idea. Although much that has happened has been faddish, some very significant, lasting developments harmonize with impending energy reforms.

The New Population Policy

The young adults of this country in the past decade have established a new population policy. The two-child family is now the national norm, and the country is on a zero population growth track. Young people are marrying later, are waiting longer to have children and are having children in fewer numbers. Although there is obviously some hedonism behind the trend toward smaller families and not a few ill-conceived notions in the experimentation with "alternative life-styles," many couples are motivated by the realization that each child born in the United States makes a profound demand on the resources of the entire world.

This new population policy will assuredly have an impact on American life. School enrollments, for example, are already leveling off. In 1972, the President's Commission on Population Growth and the American Future stated:

> After two years of concentrated effort, we have concluded that, in the long run, no substantial benefits

will result from further growth of the nation's population, rather that the gradual stabilization of our population would contribute significantly to the nation's ability to solve its problems. . . . The health of our nation does not depend on it, nor does the vitality of business nor the welfare of the average person.

A leveling off of U.S. population is a historic development that should make all of our environmental and social problems more manageable. For example, smaller families can get by with smaller cars and snugger homes and apartments. Also, less money will be needed for costly highways, schools and other public services; and more money will be available for reshaping cities, improving neighborhoods, saving open space and providing recreational opportunities.

The Success Drive Treadmill

One of the more dramatic developments since the late 1960s has been a change in attitudes towards work, money and the standard symbols of success. Increasingly smaller numbers of students and young workers believe that the job one holds or the amount of money one earns is the key to success or the measure of a person's worth. In a study released in May 1974, social researcher Daniel Yankelovich reported that America's young people for the most part hold similar attitudes toward money and work, whether or not particular individuals attended college. Nowadays, for example, fewer young people feel that hard work always pays off, and a sizable percentage—74 percent of the non-college group and

80 percent of the college segment—would welcome less emphasis on money.

These attitudes, along with a diminished drive for production and a waning appetite for consumption, are described by sociologist Amitai W. Etzioni as potential factors in slowing down the consumption of energy and changing the living habits of all Americans. He advances one of the most unlikely concepts of energy reform—living for pleasure. For indications of this new movement, he warns, don't look at hippies or executive dropouts. More significant evidence is seen in the executive who stops taking his work-laden briefcase home in the evenings and on weekends and in workers who elect early retirement.

Even though Etzioni doesn't use the phrase "think lean," he articulates the concept. A society that downgrades the priority of production and consumption has time and energy to exert its efforts towards ends that are aesthetically more rewarding to the individual—a return to craftsmanship, for instance, or increased involvement with neighborhood and community activities.

Back to the Soil

The allure of a simpler way of life has become one of the more celebrated themes of the youth counterculture that in the past half-dozen years has experimented with communal living arrangements. Most people, however, born and raised in metropolitan areas, are not prepared for the harshness and uncertainty of farming or a rustic existence. In most cases, members of the new "whole earth" cult learned quickly that they couldn't survive without help. But while they failed to prove that everyone can move to a farm, they did establish a refreshing new attitude that attached prestige to working with one's hands, raising one's own food and being generally self-sufficient. Country living, not as a leisurely country gentleman, but country working and living as an alternative lifestyle, has a new status and has lost much of the stigma it had received in recent decades when the emphasis was on metropolitan living.

This trend has brought about a resurgence of interest in gardening and canning. While the unusual increase in the sale of garden vegetable seeds and the almost-forgotten canning supplies obviously doesn't mean all Americans are attempting to return to a more agrarian style of life, it does indicate there is a need to feel more self-sufficient. A family feels that it has gained some control of its life by actually growing some of its own food, even if it is only a modest addition to the family dining table.

There is, of course, only minimal energy or financial savings in a small garden, but the harvesting of the vegetables and fruit, the cooking and sealing, the labeling and storing of the newly canned jars on a pantry or basement shelf is a family event and is in itself a recognition that not every part of the American lifestyle has to, or should be, mass produced and nationally distributed. Another benefit not to be overlooked is that canning time with steaming kitchens and the tantalizing smells of bubbling jellies or vegetables, and paraffin seals and heavy Mason jars is a pleasant reminder of a simpler, more independent way of life.

The Bicycle Scale

In retreating from the frenetic pace of American life, it isn't possible or practical for most people to live the small town, country life. But it is possible to slow down, and to scale down; to become less dependent on the highly mechanized systems and begin to place greater reliance on smaller, diverse efforts to provide the services and products of a society that has chosen to relax its pace and reduce its appetites.

No society remains static. It is ever-changing and offering new opportunities. Bicycling, partly because of the ecology movement, partly because of the energy crisis, and partly because of a renewed interest in physical fitness and personal health, has had a dramatic boom in America. In 1972, for example, bicycles outsold automobiles for the first time and they continue to sell at a solid rate (15.3 million in 1973), creating whole new areas of demand and business opportunities not previously anticipated. Moreover, one out of every two bikes is purchased for use by an adult.

Despite the lack of facilities and a defined role for the bicycle, it is already making an impact on the changing American lifestyle. One of the new business opportunities that has grown with the bicycle is the need for small, individually-owned-and-operated bicycle shops throughout the country. With a small initial investment, a modest store front and space, an individual can enter a business that is proving to be both personally rewarding and financially successful.

The self-fulfillment derived from owning and operating small businesses like bicycle shops is evidenced in the number of people who are going into related pursuits, such as plant shops and craft cooperatives, which stimulate a renewed interest in crafts and art. There will be other opportunities (in areas most people have not yet anticipated) that can be suited to a more realistic scale of life.

Adjustments and Accommodations

In coming to terms with the realities of energy shortages, we must develop a lifestyle based on an understanding that the earth's resources are limited and that we must draw upon them within a framework of conservation. Success will depend on the overall willingness of adults and children alike to have leaner, more sensible expectations about what the good life entails.

The good life doesn't have to be keyed to an ideology of ever-increasing production and consumption. Living leaner will be more meaningful because we will also be forced to examine what is really important in terms of individual and family satisfactions.

As energy scarcities reshape our lives within the next few years, Americans will see impressive changes in mobility and transportation, the buildings in which they live and their neighborhoods and communities. Industry will also become more thrifty in its production techniques and its use of resources. And we hope increased citizen participation and the commitment to a frugal lifestyle will make our lives richer and more rewarding. For most Americans the new era will provide an opportunity to enjoy life as they live it and to measure success in the simple things that make them feel that it's good to be alive.

chapter six

RESTORING TRANSPORTATION OPTIONS

"The jet knows only two places—where it takes off and where it lands. It is like the swift freeways of Los Angeles—passing through Watts, ignorant of its existence.

I must choose trains in order to allow myself time to relate to that earth and the men who changed it, just a few feet outside my window in the passing weathers."

—Ray Bradbury

Transportation—getting back and forth to work, exchanging goods and services and spending recreational and leisure time—is one of the dominant shaping factors in any society. In the United States in the 1970s, the transportation choice is singular: It is the automobile and truck, with the airplane as the only long-distance alternative.

Each day, millions of motorized vehicles roll across a vast network of expressways, turnpikes, highways, roads, streets, alleys and lanes. So much of the landscape has been paved to accommodate our rubber-wheeled society that there is one linear mile of paved road for every square mile of land in the United States.

Since the end of World War II, the airplane and, even more, the automobile and truck have upset a once-efficient, balanced national transportation system of trains, trolleys, buses and intraurbans. Aided by a massive, federally financed highway building program and the rush to the suburbs, the automobile and its highly polluting, energy-wasteful engine reign supreme.

In 1945, this country had a balanced transportation system. The transit lines of the United States—railroads, subway and elevated trains, trolleys and buses—were a substantial part of that system and carried 23 billion passengers. By 1973, however, the same forms of public transportation carried just over 6 billion, a little more than one-fourth of the first total, even though the national population had grown from about 140 million in 1945 to over 200 million in 1970.

The United States had one of the best and most varied urban transit systems, and perhaps the finest overall railroad services in the world, at the end of World War II. There was an interlocking network of complementary services in which the motorcar actually reinforced the other segments of the system and made it work more flexibly. One of the initial benefits of the auto was the construction of "farm-to-market" roads. In the beginning the car was a luxury, but it had promise and each state and city formed "good roads" committees to promote highway building. The necessary building of better roads and the improvement of existing ones certainly strengthened the overall transportation system. Such construction opened up neglected sections of the country to commerce and recreation. So long as the automobile functioned as part of a balanced transportation system, it was beneficial. It became a destructive force only when the decisions were made that gave it dominance.

Through World War II, the cities were so compact and mass transit services so widespread that 85 percent of the traveling public used public transportation, walked or bicycled. Even in major cities, most people lived in closely knit neighborhoods convenient to public transportation and could walk to work or get there by bus or trolley. Part of the daily commute was a healthy morning or evening walk to work or to the trolley stop. The cities were quieter, lacking the pounding din of automobiles and trucks. The air was generally cleaner, and it was safer for children to walk or ride bicycles on the streets.

The misguided land-use zoning of the later decades that would rigidly separate stores and shops from homes and apartments was not in effect then. Shops, markets, grocers, butchers, shoe repairmen and the extensive array of necessary stores and services were also nearby, or were an easy walk for a child sent on an errand for a loaf of bread or a spool of thread.

For some of the basic necessities that might not be located in the immediate neighborhood, there was a system of delivery boys who brought groceries that had been ordered by telephone; roaming fruit and vegetable hucksters in from the country with fresh produce; milkmen and laundrymen on regular routes; and even itinerant twentieth-century tinkers who could "repair anything."

Many people had cars, but most received only limited use since the public transportation systems worked so well. Cars existed more for weekend and pleasure riding, or for an occasional long trip to visit a relative or take a vacation. To use an automobile for commuting to work was out of the ordinary. The city bus and trolley systems were clean and efficient; for longer trips, trains ran on schedule, were inexpensive and serviced an extensive network of cities, large and small.

The spine of this effective, balanced transportation system was the railroad. It reached its peak during World War II. In 1944, freight traffic in ton-miles stood at two-and-one-half times the level of 1938 and passenger miles had increased fourfold. About 100 billion passenger miles were logged that year. From that point on, the role of railroads declined steadily. Even though they still carry about 40 percent of the nation's freight between cities, passenger service was a slowly dying mode of travel until Amtrak and the 1973 energy crisis sparked a renewal of interest in rail travel. The automobile is now the major carrier of people between cities, accounting for 85 percent of this traffic, while railroads and buses together account for only 3 percent, with 10 percent going to airplanes. The loss of passengers to airplanes is further evidenced in the fact that at the end of the war the railroads had totaled about 100 billion passenger miles, while they totaled less than 10 billion passenger miles in 1972. Air travel during that same period showed a dramatic increase, from 5 billion passenger miles in 1945 to 125 billion in 1972.

When economics and the proliferation of automobiles induced the railroads to junk passenger services and to concentrate instead on freight haulage, the most efficient element of the transportation system was smashed. Railroads have always been very thrifty users of energy. Trucks, cars and airplanes have never been in their league. At the end of the war, however, the railroads were permitted to wither as the country pursued the belief that cheap oil meant a better transportation system could be built around the car, truck and airplane. These forms of transportation could only fill the void with substantial public assistance. The federal government heavily subsidized private transportation through massive highway building—national in scale and at taxpayer expense.

The nation made a major commitment to the motorized vehicle and the airplane as soon as the austerity of World War II was over. We quickly transformed the industrial system from wartime to peacetime production. From the onset of the Great Depression in 1929 until 1945, the construction of homes and autos had been repressed, but now the national goal was full employment. The fighting men returned home hoping to fulfill dreams of owning an automobile and a home on their own plot of land.

Detroit and the petroleum industry were eager to supply the automobile boom, and the Federal Housing Authority and veterans' low mortgage benefits helped make the money available for the construction of new homes and subdivisions on the fringes of the cities.

During the war, the federal government had built a giant aircraft industry and had trained thousands of men to repair and fly a new generation of aircraft. At the end of the war, this industry was ready to make the easy transition to civilian, commercial travel. The airplane had proven its usefulness and safety during the war, and a more affluent population was willing and ready to turn to this form of transportation. Nearly every city wanted to have its own prestige airport, and substantial federal subsidies were invested in facilities for new air terminals, which encouraged commercial aviation.

By the end of the 1960s, the U.S. was consuming more energy for air travel than it had used to transport all of its goods in trains and trucks in the 1930s. Passenger goods were increasing almost 15 percent each year, the air transport industry envisioned a doubling of air travel every five years, and such hub cities as Miami, Los Angeles, Dallas and Atlanta were building or planning superjet ports to accommodate soaring future growth needs.

The ultimate commitment was made to the automobile in 1956—when Congress passed and President Dwight D. Eisenhower signed a law creating the 40,000-mile, high-speed Interstate Highway System. The legislation successfully made its way through Congress after proponents argued that it would vastly improve transportation facilities and that it was necessary for the evacuation of cities in the event of atomic attack. The weakness of the latter argument should be evident to anyone who has seen stand-still rush-hour traffic congestion in most American cities. One wonders how it would ever be possible to totally evacuate an entire city when daily partial evacuations have so much difficulty.

The passage of this highway building legislation signified the nation's total commitment to the automobile and the truck. From the war years on, federal subsidies went to airplanes and rubber-wheeled travel. Virtually nothing went to railroads or to public transportation. It wasn't Congress's intention to destroy the railroads or to disrupt urban mass transit systems. The American people simply wanted rubber wheels and silver wings. It all seemed to make sense. Building cars, trucks and planes provided millions of jobs, and an increase in the use of cheap petroleum helped soak up a glut of oil. Few people could envision the chaos that would result.

The Highway Act of 1956 created the Highway Trust Fund, a pork-barrel bonanza for highway engineers, contractors, pavers and all the subsidiary interests who would thereafter form the highway lobby, one of the most powerful pressure groups in Washington or in any state capital in the nation. The highway builders, unfortunately, were short-sighted. They knew how to build an American

Appian way, but they had little insight into the problems of urban and regional development. Without the capacity to deal with the social problems produced by running an expressway through a fragile neighborhood community, they became the unwitting shapers of the national destiny.

Designed solely to increase the speed and volume of traffic, the expressways avoided cities and towns as they bulldozed the countryside. Where cities were penetrated, the builders destroyed the neighborhoods, separated cities with walls of concrete, and used up some of the most valuable scenic space. Examples of this intrusion on natural beauty and destruction of urban amenities can be seen in nearly every major American city—along the San Francisco waterfront or the Chicago lake front, for example, and in areas of Fairmount Park in Philadelphia.

With $26 billion allotted to the states to be spent over twenty years (federal funding accounted for 90 percent, state contributions for the other ten percent), it was frontier days for the land speculators, real estate developers and the automobile salesmen. With it all came an unprecedented demand on resources, petroleum, concrete and steel.

Revenues from federal excise taxes on gasoline and other auto-related products were generating nearly $6 billion annually into the fund by the beginning of 1970. At the same time, all levels of government—federal, state and local—were spending more than $20 billion each year on highways. The trucking industry was the major beneficiary of the new highspeed highways. Often running parallel to railroads lines, this new system of roads gave trucks the competitive advantage. With the interstate expressways, the trucks no longer were slowed down by the old state and federal routes that forced them to travel through the center of virtually every city or small town. In bypassing the towns, trucks could make impressive time traveling from point to point, and the trucking industry grew tremendously.

It has been speculated that if a fraction of the original $26 billion in the Highway Trust Fund had been spent revitalizing the railroads—repairing and replacing obsolete equipment, fixing roadbeds and improving passenger facilities—that trains could have continued to make a major contribution to U.S. transportation. Now the major objection to trains and other forms of public transportation is that they have been allowed to decay and become unsightly and uncomfortable.

With all the money committed to highways, it was no surprise that between 1958 and 1968, 858 intercity passenger trains disappeared, including the legendary 20th Century Limited, the Lark and the Chief. Then, in the spring of 1971, in one swift stroke of the pen, the newly formed Amtrak Corporation, a public/private corporation created by Congress to run national passenger service, discontinued 50 percent of the nation's remaining rail service.

The automobile and the truck became pacesetters of the national economy. The internal combustion engine established a standard of independence and personal mobility that is now an inseparable part of the way this nation works, lives and plays—from the rumbling tractor trailer rigs to the roaring trail-bikes and bouncing dune buggies.

Throughout the day heavy trucks lumber back and forth across the country on short hauls or transcontinental treks, carrying everything from eggs to heavy machinery. They carry citrus fruit from California and Florida, cotton from the South, wheat and meat from Kansas and Illinois, coal from Pennsylvania and West Virginia, gasoline from New Jersey and Ohio refineries, wine from New York, beer from Wisconsin, textiles from North Carolina, medicines from Delaware.

In the transportation of goods and services, trucks are dominant. Although trains still carry a significant share of the nation's freight, as to a much lesser extent do airplanes, it is the diesel-driven truck that moves the goods of the nation. Since the end of World War II, railroad freight has increased only 17 percent, while truck freight hauling went up a stunning 222 percent.

In the average household, most products, from the food on the dining table to the household furniture to the linens and clothing to the numerous accessories and appliances, come into the home only after being brought to local stores through a complex production and distribution system using trucks of all sizes and shapes. Unlike prewar America, very few of these items come from the homeowners' local community or immediate area. Because it is widely believed nearly all modern industry must grow to a national scale to compete effectively, centralization of production and distribution often creates a situation where a product grown or produced in one community must travel many truck miles to a processing-distribution point before being brought back into the community for sales in local shops.

It is also possible that a person can live a few miles from produce farms and a few blocks from a supermarket and still buy vegetables that come from mass-produced, machine-processed factories in the fields hundreds of miles away. The produce grown in nearby fields will likely end up in a canned or frozen product that the local resident can only buy after a truck has moved it to a processor, then to a distributor, to the supermarket warehouse and finally back to the local community store.

The extent of the nation's dependence on trucking was apparent in the winter of 1974, when many truckers pulled their rigs off the highways to protest the rising prices of diesel fuel. Their action provoked immediate concern about shortages of basic commodities—especially food products—and set off small flurries of panic-buying and hoarding on the part of people who correctly assumed that without trucks the grocery stores and cupboard shelves would quickly empty.

While trucks feed and service the nation, it is the automobile that is the ever-present companion, status symbol and source of entertainment and pride. No movie cowboy ever had as much affection for his horse as many Americans have for their automobiles. Billions of dollars are invested in the care, parking, polishing, repairing and insuring of automobiles.

The motorized economy used up nearly 25 percent of all the energy burned in the country, with half that amount going for the automobile alone. This is a staggering energy commitment; the U.S. uses more energy for transportation than all except one or two other nations use for all purposes. With oil prices reaching ever-higher levels and the stability of supply seriously in doubt, it is obvious that the nation's transportation habits must be significantly changed. It would be ridiculous to even begin thinking about energy conservation or petroleum self-sufficiency without examining the nation's grossly wasteful transportation system and instituting plans to make revolutionary changes that will rebalance the system, offering a more efficient range of alternatives.

The postwar growth trends in transportation and petroleum production both neared a peak in the 1970s. Crude oil production reached an apparent all-time peak in November of that year, but Detroit's auto builders were apparently oblivious to the significance of this development. Earlier in the year, the automotive companies reported a "confident prediction" that auto production would jump from twenty-two thousand to forty-one thousand per day by the end of the decade. The American Automobile Association, not to be outclassed, forecasted that by 1985 the number of registered autos, trucks and buses on the road would jump from 106 million to over

178 million. Eager state highway officials were esti-
mating that more than forty thousand additional
miles of freeways would be needed to handle the
expected surge in traffic.

The increase in fuel consumption grew to such
outlandish proportions that by 1973 the United
States needed more than 13 million barrels of crude
petroleum every day just to feed the appetites of the
rubber-wheeled fleet. With about half a barrel of
crude oil ending up as gasoline after refining, automobile traffic was creating a demand for an average
of more than 6.5 million barrels of gasoline a day.

In the twenty-five years between 1945 and 1970,
the number of motor vehicles on the road more than
tripled, from 30 million cars and trucks to over 100
million, and the total miles of highway traveled in
the United States increased more than four times,
from 250 billion miles a year in 1945 to over 1.1
trillion miles as we entered the 1970s. During this
same period, automobiles and trucks increased in
weight and horsepower, and fuel efficiency sharply
declined. In 1945, the typical automobile could
travel up to 20 miles on a gallon of gas. But less than
twenty-five years later, the newer, much heavier machines were consuming one gallon of gas for every
11 or 12 miles traveled.

The cost of all this was greater than the total
economies of many countries. In 1971, for example,
it was estimated that expenditures for private auto
transportation in the United States—new car production, upkeep, oil and gasoline, finance charges, in-

surance and tires on passenger cars alone—generated about $100 billion of the nation's Gross National Product. This was equivalent to the total economic output of Canada that year, and greater than the entire Gross National Product of all the Scandinavian countries combined (Norway, Sweden, Denmark and Finland).

The importance of motorized vehicles to the economy (one of six jobs are related to the auto industry) and lifestyle of the United States cannot be overstated. The American megasprawl, which both fed the growth of the automobile and could not have overrun the countryside without the automobile, now cannot exist without it.

With singular dependence on cars and trucks crippling other forms of transportation, more than 80 percent of the national population is now dependent on the automobile for getting to and from work. With more than half of the cars carrying only one occupant, this is an unforgivable waste of gasoline.

The predominant use of the automobile in short-distance trips, generally inching along in stop-and-go, gasoline-burning commuting, dramatizes the postwar separation between workplace and residence and the absence of adequate means of public transportation.

Besides the automobile's contribution as a means of getting to work and to the stores—in modern suburban communities most stores and shops are now situated far from residential neighborhoods—there is the automobile's luxury, leisure and recreational value. In fact, a third of all the miles a family puts on its car is purely for social and recreational activities. This extensive portion of the approximately ten thousand miles a year an average family logs on the odometer is not for long trips to the national parks or to Disneyland. It is, instead, for casual visits or just for pleasure riding. More than 12 percent of all the miles traveled is added on just in visiting relatives and friends, a total that is higher even than the 7.6 percent of the mileage added in shopping.

That 12 percent hightlights yet another aspect of the population growth patterns of the United States of the past 30 years. When most people lived within walking distance or an easy trolley ride from where they worked or shopped, it was easy to visit a coworker or relative in the evening or for Sunday dinner. At that time, a person's friends had generally been known since childhood and few moved far from the old neighborhoods.

In the automobile–suburban culture of the 1970s, however, parents, children and other relatives and friends are spread across the country. Coworkers employed by the same firm in the city now generally live in as many different locations throughout the greater metropolitan area as it is possible to live. It is not unusual for two friends who work together to live at opposite ends of the metropolitan area, requiring an automobile trip of 50 miles or more just to get together for a Sunday barbeque. Yet most Americans have been so committed to the cheap gasoline–automobile lifestyle that they don't question driving such distances for a party or just for a chat.

It is this unquestioning attitude that took a heavy toll on the once-thriving public transportation systems. The result has been a model of transportation extravagance. The single-minded concentration of money and resources on the automobile has also been at a terrible cost in human life—more than fifty thousand people are killed annually and more than 3 million are injured or maimed for life.

It took the shock waves of the Arab embargo to drive home the point that the country was living beyond its energy budget and that the plans of the airlines and the automakers were outlandish. The fuel shortages not only produced curtailments in airline schedules and massive unemployment in the auto factories, they also punctured all the extravagant growth myths nurtured by these industries. The looming shortages—and the new quadrupled prices for imported petroleum imposed by the oil producers' cartel—pointed up the deficiencies of our present transportation system: big cars are economically impractical; the U.S. has too many highways and travel facilities; the nation has been tragically shortsighted in forcing its railroads and transit companies to discontinue services; and the oil companies lack the integrity to meet the petroleum needs projected for the nation.

In sum, the fuel shortages and the revelation that the oil industry was probably at or near its peak level of performance served notice on the American people that they had come to a turning point and needed to move expeditiously toward a diverse, highly efficient transportation system. The role of the auto, the airplane and the truck will have to diminish as the capacity of reinvigorated railroads and stronger systems of public transportation are developed. The transportation system must be returned to balance in a society that learns that driving less and relying on public transportation more is a better way to live.

Once we have committed ourselves to trimming waste, the first order of business will be to reduce automobile weight and gas consumption. As Henry Ford II has already acknowledged, "the big car as we know it today is on its way out." The fuel economy of the next generation of automobiles must at least be doubled this decade to 25 miles per gallon. With over 40 percent of the petroleum used in the country devoted to motor vehicle transportation, the savings of such an increase in efficiency will be dramatic.

Two changes could stretch the remaining U.S. petroleum resources twice as far and reduce gasoline consumption by over 50 percent within a decade. To begin, Congress must legislate the sizes and weight of new automobiles and reduce the average weights and horsepower by about 60 percent within five years. A society that is using up its oil at a frightening rate cannot afford oversized cars.

The second change involves the development of

a whole generation of cars. It no longer makes sense, if it ever did, for every U.S. motorcar to be built to run at high speeds. The type of vehicle needed is a little runabout, or "commuter" mini-car, which might be designed for an efficiency of at least 80 miles per gallon and be used strictly for in-town and short-haul travel. Such fuel thrift is not beyond our capability. The Japanese already have a 50 horsepower automobile on the market that competes with the present generation of cars; in addition to low prices, it offers fuel economy of about 40 miles per gallon at 50 miles per hour.

While such mini-cars will be limited to runabout and commuter use, their economy and size would permit enough personal mobility in an energy-short economy and add a measure of versatility in urban centers clogged with unwieldy, high-polluting cars. Some of these autos might be electric, if adequate batteries can be developed, but a varied propulsion fleet would be preferable in order not to put an intolerable load on the electric utilities.

At present more than 50 percent of auto trips are less than 5 miles in length and almost 90 percent of all auto trips are under 15 miles in length. Small cars would be ideal for such travel, and, once the size and speeds of other cars are reduced, small cars would be sufficiently safe for regular short-haul auto travel as well. Since more than 65 percent of all trips made by automobiles are short runs involving only one or two people, vehicles especially designed for this purpose are more practical and efficient.

The automobile industry has been unresponsive to energy-saving innovations. Although the radial tire, developed in 1948, has been standard equipment in Europe for years because it allows fuel savings, has a longer life and grips the road better, the domestic auto manufacturers have only recently adopted its advantages. After promoting optional luxuries such as factory-installed air conditioning and automatic transmissions, which reduce fuel economy by about 1.5 miles per gallon apiece on an intermediate car, Detroit suddenly "discovered" that the radial tire saved about 10 percent of the fuel consumption. After fighting emissions controls for air pollution with whining persistence and claims of reduced fuel economy for years, General Motors suddenly "discovered" that the atrociously low mileage performance on their 1974 automobiles would be improved more by the installation of a catalytic converter for pollution control in 1975 than by all the gadgets specifically designed to improve fuel economy.

The lessons of the waning of the Petroleum Era and the increased scarcity of resources are slowly finding their way into Detroit's executive suites. In 1973, more than 40 percent of the cars produced had large, fuel-thirsty, eight-cylinder engines. It is particularly ironic that the new requirements now being dictated by the energy crisis harken back to Henry Ford's original prescription: efficiency, durability, and mass availability. And General Motors— the company that introduced a new marketing strategy of annual model changes and continual stylistic improvements in their cars in order to capture the transportation market that Ford had preempted with its unchanging, long-lasting products—now seems unable to adapt to the realities of a new era. While one ex-General Motors executive works on the production of an 80-miles-per-gallon "commuter car," the present management of General Motors is stubbornly refusing to accept the end of cheap, plentiful gasoline and is aiming to achieve a very modest average of about 15 miles per gallon on all their cars. Caught well behind in the race to produce efficient, small, durable automobiles, General Motors still envisions a transportation system dominated by the automobile and the truck. Unfortunately for the country, the GM attitude still sets the trend for the industry.

Rather than increasing efficiency, versatility, and mobility, the singular reliance on oversized, inefficient motor vehicles is slowing down the very people and goods that they were designed to move about speedily and cheaply. The federal government must encourage changes by establishing transportation priorities and directing the investment of sufficient monies into alternate forms of transportation. It is time to end the building of new highways and concentrate on maintaining existing roadways. The present highway system of about 3.7 million miles will be adequate.

As the influence of the automobile within the urban area wanes, every opportunity should be taken to emphasize the role of the pedestrian. Easy access via foot to workplaces, entertainment, shops and recreational opportunities should be facilitated. Pedestrian malls within cities, the blocking off of some streets to all traffic, and the creation of well-traveled pathways should take precedence over the laying down of more concrete roadways and parking lots. Whether the benefits are measured in energy saved, pollution diminished, the reintroduction of human eyes and ears into city street life, increased commercial activity, the healthy exercise of the daily walk, or the simple ambiance and civility that comes with bustling street life, strolling and cycling require more sensitive investments and planning than highways.

While one attraction of such "shoeleather routes" is that they exemplify the human scale which any transportation system must have, the bicycle is an even more energy-efficient form of individual transport. In the last several years, the bicycle has shed its adolescent image and become an important element in the new American lifestyle. If 15 percent of the funds which are collected for highway use were invested in urban bikeways, there is no reason why up to 20 percent of the daily "commuter traffic" in many cities could not be accomplished on foot or on two wheels. Already, in many cities venturesome workers, carrying briefcases, can be seen weaving their way through downtown commuter traffic on bicycles, beating their V-8-powered neighbors through the congestion at a fraction of the cost in energy or in fuel. On weekends or vacations, entire families can enjoy long-distance outings, and young couples can combine wine, bread, and bike trips. Whether it was the heart specialist Dr. Paul Dudley White's endorsement of bicycle riding as a healthy exercise or the racer's enthusiasm for competition and speed that stimulated public interest, the bicycle in America is no longer a children's toy. Once separate bikeways are built, even the suburban housewife may choose the bicycle over the station wagon for a quick trip to the store.

Some states have already shown what can be done if Congress will only allocate funds for bike facilities of all kinds. Wisconsin has a bike path which spans the entire 300-mile width of the state, and Oregon has been using 1 percent of its gas tax receipts and federal highway funds for bike paths and foot trails.

Arlington County, Virginia, a compact urban county across the Potomac River from Washington, D.C., has recognized the transportation value of the bicycle in connecting parks, schools, libraries and residential, shopping, employment and entertainment centers by projecting an 80-mile, several-million-dollar bikeway project that would connect most parts of this 25-square-mile county. With more than 40 percent of Arlington County's residents working within the county, this network is viewed as an attractive means of going to and from work. Already the county requires inclusion of bicycle parking space in all new apartment and office building construction. In a time of energy scarcities, if at least $1 billion were allocated each year for five years for installing adequate bikeways in metropolitan areas the return would be enormous. While the construction costs for building an expressway vary from $1 million a mile in rural areas to $10 million a mile in the city, the cost of a bikeway can vary from $8,000 to $18,000 a mile. The bicycle, in other words, is more than forty times more efficient than the automobile.

Since the creation of the Highway Trust Fund in 1956, federal assistance for highways has totaled more than $65 billion and presently exceeds $5 billion a year. In contrast, the federal government has spent less than $3 billion in assisting urban transit systems since 1965; and since the beginning of the direct transit aid program legislated by Congress in 1970, the yearly outlay of federal monies has only exceeded $870 million in the fiscal year 1974. With a quick phase out of further federal assistance to new highway construction, spending priorities in the transportation field should now be reversed, and $5 billion of Highway Trust Fund monies should be granted annually to states and cities for improvements in a wide range of mass transit programs.

Since the end of World War II, and especially in the past decade, the urban public transit industry has been in economic decline. Although the fares have kept pace with the Consumer Price Index, patronage has not grown rapidly enough to offset operating cost increases.

Even considering the mounting expense of automobile ownership, the debilitating frustration of the daily commute on clogged highways and the difficulty in finding parking places in the overcrowded central city, the average American, given the choice, will choose the automobile over the bus or subway. As a result, more and more public transit systems are operating in the red and many privately owned ones have either gone out of business or have sold out to the municipalities they served. As a stopgap measure, others have cut back services, increased fares or done both. Still others operate under government subsidies. All the fare increases, subsidies and capital grants are only temporary respites in the seemingly relentless steady decline of the public transit systems.

The rapid growth of urban populations outside the central cities in which most mass transit systems are based resulted in a corresponding decline in the availability and use of public transportation services. From 1960 to 1970, for example, population growth outside the central cities increased by 33.5 percent as against 1.5 percent in the central cities. In 1970, the nation's suburban population actually exceeded the city population by 14 million. The density of the suburbs is low, and the increase in department stores, theaters, restaurants and other shops and sources of entertainment make it unnecessary for the suburbanite ever to travel into the city unless he works there (and even that necessity is becoming rarer as more firms relocate in suburban areas). The move of industry and business to the suburbs wasn't a boon to energy efficiency. In many cases, relocation forced many employees to circumnavigate the central city or force their way through it simply to get to work. This low-density, formless suburban spread made it impossible for conventional public transportation systems to operate profitably.

In 1973, the Environmental Protection Agency identified thirty-seven metropolitan areas in the United States where exhausts from overconcentrations of motor vehicles threaten the health of the population of entire cities. In order to obtain clean air in such areas, there will have to be a reduction in automobile travel, since the auto is responsible for more than half the nation's air pollution problem and as high as 80 percent in some metropolitan areas. A reduction in air pollution thus fits in well with the requirements of the energy crisis. It will necessitate a shift away from automobiles to more efficient public transit systems, including buses and rapid transit, and such a shift will decrease traffic congestion and conserve large amounts of fuel—for in urban passenger travel, the automobile uses from two to three times as much fuel as mass transit to move one individual.

Just as mass transit systems throughout the nation must be strengthened, and experimental development of electric trolleys and monorails hastened, so must there be a resurgence of intercity rail passenger service. Rapid Metroliner service in the high-density corridor between New York and Washington has shown the profitability and competitiveness of rail passenger traffic (even though the rail bed on this line is in bad shape). While improvements in the Metroliner trackage will be expensive, the passenger traffic is already there to assure long-term profitability, and the likelihood of increased population congestion and diminished fuel supplies makes the Metroliner's future that much brighter.

Immediate profitability cannot be the single criterion for increasing intercity rail service in other areas of the country. During the energy shortage of 1973–74, ridership on the Amtrak passenger lines increased 30 percent. Because of the long deterioration in rail lines and equipment which form the capital base of the National Railroad Passenger Corporation, however, Amtrak was ill-prepared to handle the influx of intercity rail passengers. Instead of using the dilapidated condition of the long-distance track and equipment which it has inherited and leased from the private rail companies as an argument to close down further intercity rail lines, the leadership of Amtrak should be seeking new modern equipment—such as high-speed air cushion trains—to introduce into the urban corridors, which are going to require this option as oil depletion and air pollution continue.

On long-distance passenger lines, high-speed trains are certainly competitive with buses, conserve a third of the energy used by an automobile and are nearly three times as efficient as the airplane.

As for air travel in an energy-efficient, thrifty society, airplanes should be reserved for long-distance, cross-country and overseas traffic. Since the airline industry is presently heavily regulated and subsidized by the federal government, the only competition which occurs on most routes concerns in-flight movies and stewardesses' fashions. Unnecessary duplication of flight schedules, which is merely a convenience and an anachronism from an earlier era of real competition, should be eliminated. In fact, no airline flight should leave the ground unless it is at least 80 percent full.

The use of airplanes to haul freight across the country is unessential and, without a valid emergency such as the delivery of a perishable drug, constitutes a tremendous squandering of fuel and should be discontinued. Various studies indicate that the use of an airplane to deliver freight is anywhere from 62 to 125 times as wasteful as delivering the same amount of goods the same distance by train.

Long-distance trucks are also extremely inefficient in the delivery of freight and add six times the amount of pollution into the air while using six times more diesel fuel to do the same task than a train. Although railroads still carry some 40 percent of intercity freight traffic in the nation, the policy should be to place virtually all freight going long distance on the trains and reserve short-haul deliveries, where versatility is required and engine efficiency can be improved, to trucks.

It's a certainty that no one ever paused to consider that the train was more energy-efficient per passenger mile than the airplane or the automobile. The train was and still is the only civilized way to travel, but when speed became the only criterion and the railroads themselves lost interest in passenger travel a human adventure gave way to the high-speed unreality of jet travel at 30,000 feet or automobile travel at 80 miles per hour. A trip is now simply a point to point race; distance and time are annoyances to be cut as short as possible.

The reforms and new priorities needed to make a railroad resurgence possible are simple and straight-forward. To begin, Amtrak should be given what-ever subsidies are needed to modernize U.S. rail service.

Americans who visit Europe or Japan are often amazed at the smooth, comfortable, efficient, high-speed rail passenger services there. These trains often hit speeds as high as 150 miles per hour, and they travel on modern roadbeds with prestressed concrete cross-ties, continuous welded steel tracks and virtu-ally no grade crossings.

The ride on these trains is effortless and frequently one of the more pleasurable travel experiences a vacationer has. They are relatively inexpensive, serve good food and wines and often pamper their pas-sengers. Trains are an important part of the Euro-pean and Japanese transportation picture because these countries have not committed themselves to the automobile the way the United States has. Most often the foreign railroad systems are nationalized or heavily subsidized to offer frequent, punctual and inexpensive service.

By contrast, Amtrak's highly successful New York-to-Washington,-D.C., Metroliner, though capable of speeds up to 160 miles per hour, must operate at significantly lower speeds because of the poor roadbeds, wooden crossties and numerous grade crossings. Sadly, the Metroliner tracks are less antiquated than the bulk of the nation's system.

In the years ahead, the best investment the United States can make is in the railroad sector. Borrowing from the European and Japanese experience, high-quality roadbeds and first-rate equipment should be provided, so that vastly improved performances can be achieved. If this can be accomplished only by nationalizing the railroad rights of way—or by nationalizing the weakest links of the system outright—then such steps should be taken.

Within five years the building of new highways should be phased out, and most of the funds now being funneled into roads should be spent on the revival of the rails. The federal government must finance an effort to develop a tracked air-cushion train and other new technologies that can provide 200- to 300-mile-per-hour intercity bullet trains, particularly for the densely populated urban corridors. One of the ironies of our current plight is that if the Department of Transportation had spent the $1 billion plus it squandered on the supersonic airplane proposal on this new train technology, America might very well be working right now on the first unit of the world's finest and most efficient ground transportation system. The gain in energy and environmental savings from such a program would be enormous. Obviously, if fast train travel were to cut intercity travel in half, the overall dividends for conservation would be enhanced significantly.

In the longer run, if the railroads are revived and

excellent mass transit systems are put into operation, the role of automobiles will shrink even further. Millions of Americans will turn to superior, public forms of transportation, making the automobile more and more a costly, unnecessary burden. With new urban design locating shops and stores within walking distance of most people, public transportation will become the most convenient mode of transit.

Coupling the greater use of public transportation and the lowering of horsepower for remaining automobiles, the fuel savings will be dramatic. If maximum speeds on highways are also maintained at 55 miles per hour, more than 5 million gallons of gasoline will be saved each day. The lowered speed limits will be measured in preserved human life also. When the maximum limits were reduced during the Arab embargo, highway fatalities dropped. There were, for example, 30 percent fewer highway deaths in February 1974 than in the same month of the previous year.

Obviously, better trains and public transportation, along with fewer autos, smaller cars with less horsepower, and the recognition of bicycles and the pedestrian will result in healthier, safer urban environments, will contain suburban sprawl and conserve fuel for future generations and for more basic industrial needs. Trimming wasteful transportation habits will produce a better, more efficient America. The pace will also be slower and more human, and there will be more time for people to experience a leaner, more energy-efficient lifestyle.

chapter seven

SHAPING THE HUMAN ENVIRONMENT

"As planners and architects we have been trained to look a long way ahead—or try to. Cars, skyscrapers, cities are all there to stay, but hopefully not in their present form. All is change and all is diversity, and it is our job—sometimes unpleasant—to tell what we think we see in the crystal ball and try to make out what we should do about it. What I see there now says, like a broken computer, Go slow. Go slow."

—Nathaniel A. Owings
Architect

It is a fortuitous coincidence of history that some of the most important reforms dictated by the energy crisis, such as the decreased reliance on the automobile and the building of better public transportation networks, come at a time when the nation appears to be ready to adopt wise land-use policies and begin reshaping our cities into better human environments.

It may not be possible to recreate the type of neighborhood mix—social, residential, commercial and economic—that once existed in most U.S. cities and towns across the country, but the new energy awareness will impel much better community planning and emphasize neighborhood values as our urban settings are redesigned.

Fortunately, the need to be thrifty in our use of energy coincides with the emerging consensus of city planners, urbanologists, architects and social scientists: arrangements must stress what urbanologist Jane Jacobs described in her classic work, *The Death and Life of Great American Cities,* as an "intricate and close-grained diversity of uses that give each other constant mutual support, both economically and socially." Surely there can no longer be any doubt that autos and urban sprawl, and the enormous waste of energy they entail, destroy the very conditions that make good cities and good neighborhoods possible. And clearly the solution is to design communities that focus on the neighborhood as an active, viable part of the human experience, making it an intimate place where people can live, work, shop and play.

This recognition of the centrality of human beings in urban design was the theme of the annual convention of the American Institute of Architects, who met in Washington, D.C., in 1974 to discuss "A Humane Architecture." In their meetings, they began exploring the idea that, above all else, the purpose of any structure should be to promote human values and enhance the neighborhood and the community by making the city more livable.

At their national conference the previous year, members of the AIA had acknowledged the horrendous waste of energy that is an integral part of modern architecture and decided it was time to begin to develop a program of energy conservation. It should now be excruciatingly evident that any effort to produce "humane architecture" must also be energy efficient. Buildings which are designed, constructed and operated with only a façade of life, and which are dependent on the mechanical over the human, must pay the price for this artificiality in wasted energy and diminished personal satisfactions and social relationships.

Any design which values the neighborhood concept will also emphasize energy conservation and efficiency in the arrangement of the man-made environment. More than one-third of all the energy consumed in this country is allocated to the heating, ventilating, air conditioning, and lighting of residential and commercial buildings—homes, shopping centers, stores, hotels and office buildings.

The most important initial action taken to conserve energy in residential and commercial structures in the United States is evident: think about living simpler lives and using less energy better!

Like most good ideas, the concept of a humane architecture seems so obvious that one wonders why it has been neglected so long. But in the frantic home construction and commercial building boom of the past thirty years, when U.S. "progress" was equated with statistics of new construction, the human factor, like the energy factor, was usually overlooked.

When architects finally made a concentrated study of building design, they discovered that new structures could be erected with a potential energy saving of 50 to 80 percent over present buildings, and that many older buildings could be altered to cut energy use by 25 to 50 percent. In achieving such savings, essential services need not be reduced. In many instances, as the overall arrangements are made more efficient and scaled down to take advantage of natural conditions and mesh with the surrounding environment, creative human interplay will also be increased.

With rueful hindsight, most architects are now quick to admit that modern houses and office buildings have seldom been built with the thrifty use of energy in mind. An energy exhibition prepared by New York architects in 1973 stated: "Energy waste occurs in cooling, heating, lighting, ventilation and transportation and in uses of form and material . . . . Most commercial buildings are overequipped mechanically to handle heating, cooling and ventilating loads that are universally high. Glass is used indiscriminately without sun control devices. Heating and air conditioning are often inefficient." And many of these "modern" structures are vastly underused and dehumanize their neighborhoods. The average office building is depopulated at five o'clock each evening, with the hum and whirr of the mechanical caretakers continuing throughout the night.

Like giant, plugged-in commercial appliances, these buildings rarely integrate and sustain the neighborhoods into which they intrude. Instead, they simply dominate an area. Without space for small retail establishments—theaters, restaurants and other little shops and businesses—on the street level to offer the variety of personal services necessary to maintain street life after working hours, streets around these buildings are lonely and deserted.

Built strictly as daytime, speculative investments, such structures cast a shadow of economic foreclosure on surrounding property, particularly older, lower-rent buildings and smaller residential units. Suddenly inflated land values can rezone a neighborhood and exclude a broad spectrum of people and small businesses. While the property values and taxes of the surrounding properties may rise with each additional story of the new building, the richness of life and the attraction for human activity are diminished as the delights and delicacies of the fresh produce stand and the local bistro are priced out of existence and vanish with the barber shop, the bakery and the family-owned restaurant.

In the mad rush of new construction, the concept of neighborhood—living and working and playing on a more compact, self-sufficient scale—hasn't been entirely ignored. Recognition of the need to give people a sense of community has spurred the "new town" movement in Europe and the United States—an experiment which combines efficiency with the creation of lifegiving environments.

The new town idea also recognizes that wasteful, monotonous assembly line construction is not only environmentally destructive, but could have many adverse human and social side-effects as well.

One of the earliest new towns, and one of the most impressive, is Tapiola, Finland, a community of some sixteen thousand people that was begun in 1951 as a protest against poorly planned housing projects. Six miles from downtown Helsinki, located in a lake pine forest, this town boasts a sensitive cluster of houses and apartments that gives spaciousness and a dominant human scale.

The architecture of the community is carefully adopted to the country surroundings, and more space is set aside for flowers, walkways and bikeways than is reserved for roadways and automobiles.

Two of the most important and meaningful aspects of Tapiola's scale of living are that it is a child-centered community, safe for children and their tricycles, and that each household has a neighborhood store no more than 300 yards away. Nearly 80 percent of the residents live and work in Tapiola, and those who commute to Helsinki use highly efficient public transportation.

The new town idea in the United States has borrowed heavily from this concept with the creation of self-contained satellite communities at or beyond the urban fringe. In spite of the frequent commercial bastardization of the term "new town" by some real estate developers who add a few amenities to their housing projects, the genuine new towns encompass the need for neighborhood diversity and density; a mix of employment opportunities, housing, shops, and restaurants; and community and recreational facilities.

The two most famous new towns in the United States are Reston, 20 miles from Washington, D.C., in the Virginia countryside, and Columbia, a town that grew up on a cow pasture in Maryland, 25 miles from Washington, D.C., and 12 miles from Baltimore.

The designers of both Reston and Columbia have avoided the sterile look and the "people sorting" that marred look-alike developments built for particular income and age groups in the suburbs after World War II. Rather, they have tried to create self-sufficient communities with a blend of income groups, employment opportunities, shopping, recreation, schools and other essential services built in at the beginning. The dominating concern is for both neighborhood and efficiency. Even in these towns, everyone does not live within walking distance of the various town centers, but there is, nevertheless, an attempt to promote the same feeling of belonging and common spirit which were once dominant aspects of urban life in America. While energy efficient, the shared-wall townhouses so prevalent in the new towns give each resident limited personal green space. The residents, however, share much more extensive open areas than are found in the older, unplanned suburban communities.

At their best, the new towns offer greater opportunity for a person to receive individual recognition in his community and to exercise greater control over the many things that affect his life, but as yet they have not been sufficiently successful in attracting the diverse populations and industries needed to make them a complete success. So far, new towns in the United States are generally inhabited by more affluent, younger, middle-class professional people and attract the white-collar industries. But discounting such failings, the new town movement should be encouraged by governments. Their compactness permits the more efficient use of energy and offers superior living values as well. They recognize the need for neighborhood diversity and for the comprehensive blend of social, cultural, environmental and economic factors which is missing in the average American suburb.

If we are going to stop suburban sprawl in this country and use our dwindling supply of prime land more wisely, it is important to build on the new town concept and re-create healthy neigborhoods in our core cities. Smaller, more compact homes closer to work, recreation and shops mean much less energy will be required for heating, cooling and transportation. This is the vital point where better neighborhoods and energy reforms converge. Energy shortages not only halt sprawl, they are also a mandate for close-knit, self-sufficient neighborhoods.

Fortunately, the concepts of density, self-sufficiency, neighborhood and population mix can be applied nearly everywhere. What might be described as the next step in new towns is a planned community on Franklin D. Roosevelt Island, a narrow sliver of land in New York City's East River. This "new town in town" will house 21,000 families of diverse incomes, origins and cultures.

More important, this community, like the new towns, is to be built on near-ideal human scale, and because of the density and mix of shops, restaurants, community and housing facilities, it will be highly energy efficient. Built on a unique tract of land within the country's most densely populated city, the island will have no cars but will have special accommodations for walking and bicycling and will operate free electric buses.

While the island setting obviously gives this community special advantages, the Roosevelt Island experiment of New York's farsighted Urban Development Corporation should teach valuable lessons about the inevitable intertwining of social and energy factors in any effort to deal with reclaimed tracts of land in or near the core area of great cities.

New town concepts applied within existing cities and communities can build upon the neighborhood scale and maximize the efficiencies of compactness, while providing for the commercial, cultural, industrial and educational facilities to service the diverse social and personal requirements of such an area. By using already-existing public structures and services—highways, streets, utilities, parks, schools—good design can revitalize vacant and dilapidated areas of cities and transform them into more attractive places to live, work, shop and play.

Most city rebuilding since World War II has had disastrous human and social consequences. More often than not, federally subsidized "slum clearance" and "urban renewal" projects mauled neighborhoods that worked reasonably well and made victims of the uprooted residents. These dislocations failed to recognize that even a ghetto has a social structure. In a series of articles in *The New York Times,* Harrison Salisbury argued:

> When slum clearance enters an area, it does not merely rip out slatternly houses. It uproots the people. It tears out the churches. It destroys the local business man. It sends the neighborhood lawyer to new downtown offices and it mangles the tight skein of community friendships and group relationships beyond repair.
>
> It drives the old-timers from their broken-down flats or modest homes and forces them to find new and alien quarters. And it pours into a neighborhood hundreds and thousands of new faces. . . .

Improvements in the functioning of neighborhoods will be important in making energy conservation and good urban design work together in the future. High-rise public housing projects all too often are turned into noncommunities, leading to social disorder and widespread crime: they must be rejected in favor of small-scale approach.

Over the past three decades, cities of all sizes lost much of their attractiveness as desirable places to live as millions of Americans fled in search of new homes surrounded by trees, grass and fresh air. But for all their environmental failures—noise, congestion, pollution, crime and stress—the older, more compact cities are much more efficient consumers of energy than the rest of the nation. Understanding the roots of that efficiency at a time when complex questions about stable energy supply and costs are being raised is vitally important, since the decisions made in the next few years will affect the way every American lives.

The reason older, more compact cities are more effective users of energy is the density and design which allows populations to live in proximity to shopping and work and to take advantage of convenient forms of public transportation.

Most Americans live in communities ringing the boundaries of cities where exclusivity and personally owned land are the ultimate objective. U.S. sprawl cities are unique in human history and in one sense symbolize an age-old wish fulfillment. Throughout history people have looked to the natural beauty and open spaces beyond the city walls. Men have always been attracted to the beauty and appeal of country living, and there has always been a belief that it was possible to escape the problems of the city by living in the countryside. Even in the very old Mediterranean civilizations, wealthier citizens built country villas to escape the unpleasant aspects of the cities.

In the Middle Ages, when cities established their dominant role as sustainers of civilization against alien forces because they were centers of commerce, education, the arts, humanity and public safety, they also had the same problems of waste disposal, congestion and pollution that afflict modern cities. At a time when plagues decimated substantial segments of the populace, those who could, fled to healthier environments.

By the nineteenth century, the beauty and serenity

of nature became a dominant theme in philosophy, literature and art in England, France and the United States. Here, it was prominent in the writings of James Fenimore Cooper and Henry David Thoreau and was particularly evident in the Hudson River School of painting, the first artists to depict the wonders of the American landscape. This recognition of nature as an aesthetic force likewise gave a favorable aura to country living.

Because a country home was often associated with affluence and gentility, a person who owned one acquired a measure of prestige. Yet, until the advent of the motor car and the all-out commitment to motorized transportation, it was not possible for any except the very wealthy to actually live "in the country" and commute each day to the city to work.

In general, American cities grew haphazardly and too quickly. Although they came in a number of varieties and populations, the heavy industrialization of the nation during the early 1900s turned many of the older, larger cities into dirty, ugly, unhealthy, unplanned concentrations of people. Paradoxically, while the city represents the best of man's aspirations, it also shows him at his shabbiest. While it is the location of great museums, it also features oppressive slums. While it offers opportunities for commercial success, it is often an unhealthy place to live. While it is a recreational and entertainment center, it is also a hub for crime.

The ardent desire for the nonurban life was present at the end of World War II; prosperous Americans, living in a nation richly endowed with natural resources, found that the automobile, cheap gasoline, high employment and inexpensive land on the fringes of the city offered the unique opportunity for millions of people to live in the country and work in the city. The movement was so extensive that by the 1970s the population of the suburbs exceeded the total population of the cities. The 1970 census figures show that 68.6 percent of all the people in the nation live in metropolitan areas. Of these 139.4 million people, 75.6 million, or 54 percent, live outside the central cities.

This exodus to initially more pleasant surroundings eventually created more problems than it solved and suburban living became the prime waster of U.S. energy, principally petroleum. The problems of the cities refused to be left behind, as millions of Americans became virtually nomadic; they moved farther and farther out to the next "garden community," "leisure world," or "new town." The energy demands caused by ever-longer automobile commutes and detached housing expanded, and the social and environmental issues surrounding sprawl development became a major national problem.

In spite of all of the advantages of owning a separate piece of land, the quality of life in this new form of country living never measured up to the advertising. Since most houses were constructed by builders who were not responsible for public facilities, there was a sameness to suburbia, with tedious, unimaginative streets blending together without producing any feeling of neighborhood or community. There was nothing to identify with, nothing to belong to, nothing in which to take pride—unless it was the superficiality of a crabgrass-free lawn. Because of insensitive, restrictive land-use zoning, many of these "bedroom" areas had no nearby community facilities of any kind. It was frequently impossible for an individual to stroll to the grocer for a loaf of bread, or to chat with the newsstand owner or the shoe repairman, or to stop in for a cup of coffee or a glass of beer and gossip at the local restaurant or corner bar. More often, one had no choice but to mobilize 250 horsepower just to get a pack of cigarettes.

Even before the energy shortages became apparent, the suburban migration had begun to reach its limits. Spreading cities were running out of inexpensive land upon which to expand, and governmental jurisdictions were unable to keep up with the public service demands. Los Angeles, the national model, revealed all the shortcomings of sprawl with its rising costs, pollution, and huge commuting distances. The steady erosion of basic living values caused an even further out-migration from a region that once probably had the finest overall environment in the country but is now considered the symbol of how not to urbanize.

The energy crisis thus accelerates a growing disenchantment with urban sprawl. It signals the end of an era and will force us to make our central cities better places to live. Significantly, most cities, no matter what their age, geographic location, population or configuration, use energy more efficiently than do other parts of the nation. The New York Urban Regional Planning Association, for example, has pointed out that New York City, with all its extravagant lighting and other energy demands, uses only half the energy per resident that the rest of the nation uses. The association reminds us that compactness saves energy and that the United States must once again make close-knit living arrangements attractive. In suburban areas, where most housing is detached, the residents consume three times more energy in their homes than people who live in high-density communities. The difference consists of the heating, cooling and lighting requirements of the free-standing homes.

In designing our communities, as in building a new transportation system, the watchwords for a more energy-efficient society will be "slow down, scale down." This will be particularly true in reorganizing the way we live, where we live and how we live. The energy crisis is timely because it has occurred as cheap land is running out, traffic congestion is worsening and agitation is increasing for wiser use of land and for reestablishing compact neighborhoods.

Before there can be a restructuring, to conserve resources and eliminate energy wastefulness, an understanding of community and neighborhood is necessary. In essence, a city or town is only as good as the neighborhood where the individual lives. If he lives in a good neighborhood, a person feels that he lives in a good city. Although city neighborhoods have been severely crippled by neglect and the urban exodus, it will not be possible to develop a leaner lifestyle until we again place a premium on the value of neighborhoods and make that concept an integral part of urban planning in both the renovating of older sections and in the development of new areas, both in town and in suburbia.

After World War II, the outward migration was so great that it was difficult to maintain the character of old neighborhoods. As deterioration took place, most bankers considered these changing areas a bad investment and refused to loan money to repair or renovate old buildings or to finance the small commercial establishments which made them function well. The refusal to insure inner city businesses, especially following the race riots of the mid-1960s, has left entire sections of the cities ugly and economically depressed. These decisions made it difficult for most city neighborhoods to hold together, further accelerating the flight to outlying areas. Left behind were the isolated wealthy and young married professionals in restrictive, guarded buildings and the poor and the blacks, still beset by the social problems that flared so violently in the 1960s in such places as Los Angeles, Cleveland, Detroit, Newark, and Washington, D.C. It is sometimes hard to remember that on the streets of these same cities social and commercial interaction had once established a feeling of belonging, a feeling of neighborhood, and a feeling of community. There had been intimate human interaction there, even though it was not always attractive.

Given the prevalent attitudes toward traffic congestion and the danger of cities, it is difficult to convince people that city life is rewarding and appealing. No one would rationally suggest that the suburbs be torn down and rebuilt to function better. We must work with what exists—making the cities more livable, planning new development in cities on the human scale, renovating existing buildings in the suburbs to make them less energy wasteful. This renovation of existing housing is important because by the end of the century it is likely 50 per cent of all existing buildings will still be in use.

The cities offer the best and most immediate opportunities for change since they already get the most out of the energy used. City life is diverse and unique, and once an effort is made to revitalize neighborhoods, housing and schools, there will be less reason to flee. Cities will then be seen as an attractive place to live. Concern about unsafe streets, for example, is dramatically lessened in areas that are alive with human activity and populated by people who are involved with each other's daily lives.

The cities will also be the immediate and major beneficiaries of better public transportation systems and the reduction of automobile traffic. While offering mobility and a means of escaping the city, the automobile also destroyed much of the ambiance of city life by creating an asphalt wasteland of congestion, air pollution, and overbuilt streets, highways and parking lots. With autos either banned from parts of the central cities or severely restricted, neighborhood streets will become community assets instead of sources of decay.

Before the automobile made mobility the dominant feature of the U.S. lifestyle, it was possible to be born, grow up, live and die in the same neighborhood and work there or nearby. Because it was such a vital part of the daily life, greater care was taken to maintain neighborhood stability. The neighborhood was, after all, more than just a place to live or shop or work. It was a social institution to which everyone belonged.

These diverse neighborhoods were good environments for children. Unlike many modern suburban children, the child in the old, close-knit, city neighborhoods was part of a functioning community and had useful daily contacts with shopkeepers and other adults. The adults were all surrogate teachers and authority figures who not only saw to it that children stayed out of trouble but also out of danger. The watchfulness wasn't stifling because the children understood they belonged to the neighborhood and that the neighborhood felt a responsibility for them. As teachers, the neighborhood adults offered an additional opportunity for the children to learn things they wouldn't learn just from parents and teachers.

At the 1973 Senate subcommittee hearings on children and youth, Dr. Urie Bronfenbrenner, professor of human development and family studies at Cornell University, testified about this phenomenon when he quoted from the White House Conference on Children that ". . . a host of factors conspire to isolate children from the rest of society. The fragmentation of the extended family, the separation of residential and business areas, the disappearance of neighborhoods, zoning ordinances, occupational mobility, child labor laws . . . all these manifestations of progress operate to decrease opportunity and incentive for meaningful contact between children and persons older, or younger, than themselves."

By isolating the children from the rest of society, Bronfenbrenner argued, the growth of the individual and the survival of the society is threatened. "It is primarily through observing, playing, and working with others older and younger than himself that a child discovers both what he can do and who he can become—that he develops both his ability and identity."

This dynamic interaction between adults and children still holds true in the older ethnic neighborhood, where there is a range of age and maturity and children continue to learn about the "old ways" from grandparents and older relatives and friends who live nearby, while the older people learn about the "new ways" from the children. The learning process isn't always easy or smooth, but it is always human, and it helps both the younger people and their elders to understand each other a little better, even when they do not agree.

Many of the ethnic neighborhoods have also been disrupted by the movement to the suburbs. In the past several years, however, there has been a resurgence in ethnicity and the desire to preserve the ethnic neighborhoods remaining in cities throughout the country. Organized efforts along this line are underway in such cities as Newark, Philadelphia, Baltimore, Gary, Indiana, and Milwaukee. Aware of the reluctance of banks to invest in their neighborhoods, residents are relying on their own savings and loan cooperatives, are fighting the real estate blockbusters and urban renewers, and are refusing to permit the freeway builders to bulldoze their neighborhoods. They have learned the tragic lesson that urban renewal destroys a neighborhood, and that the freeway canyons are as socially and physically impassable as broad rivers were to primitive man.

Some of this resistance to change is motivated by exclusivity and in some areas was also frequently a reaction to the fear of racial intrusions. More important, however, it represents the growing feeling that city neighborhoods are convenient, good places to live.

It isn't only in ethnic neighborhoods, however, that people are fighting to protect community values. Active neighborhood groups and community organizations in black areas as well as white upper-middle-class areas have been forming over the past ten years to take stands against ill-conceived freeways and other projects they believe would harm their environments.

In New York City, in the spring of 1974, neighborhood leaders came before the New York City Planning Commission to prevent such garish fast-food operations as McDonald's, Burger King, Kentucky Fried Chicken and other franchise establishments like them from establishing branches in local shopping areas. Confronted by such strong community opposition, McDonald's withdrew plans for an outlet in New York's Greenwich Village and was hampered in building four units on the Upper East Side.

During the same period, a similar battle was won by neighborhood forces in Washington, D.C., when a family-owned restaurant in a graceful, European-style area of small shops, bars and restaurants on upper Connecticut Avenue, with nearby residential streets, decided to sell out to Gino's, an East Coast fast-food chain.

Whether the protests and neighborhood victories in Washington and New York City were based on ulterior motives is of little importance. Each protester undoubtedly had his own reason—distaste for mass-produced food, opposition to corporate power, fear of litter, concern for property values, or repugnance to the plastic commercialism such businesses represent.

What was significant was that different groups were concerned enough about the quality of life offered by their neighborhoods to fight winning battles against powerful financial interests seeking to exploit them. If cities are going to become more livable, their neighborhoods do not have to accept destructive freeways, blockbusting, wrecking-ball urban renewal projects, or the intrusions of fast-buck franchisers or "developers."

If such a design revolution, keyed to energy thrift, can make our cities more natural and human places to live, so can the suburbs be reshaped into identifiable neighborhoods with adjacent shops and public facilities that supersede today's shopping centers with their yawning, meaningless parking lot environments.

As the sprawl gaps are filled with cluster housing and townhouses, there will be many opportunities to turn "bedroom" suburbs into real communities interlaced with sidewalks and bicycle paths for young and old alike. Likewise, the coming of commuter cars and convenient public transportation will change the pace and scale of suburban living and encourage citizens to put down roots again as their daily lives increase human interaction and promote community involvement.

Not only can the neighborhood model of relatively self-sustaining communities bring additional life, color and variation to the suburbs, energy efficiency is built into the modified "new town" idea of compact diversity. In this type of concentration, less can certainly be more. Less public expense for meandering streets and utility lines permits more public investment in bikeways, walkways and green space. Less need to use machine horsepower for nonessential tasks within easy walking distance allows more petroleum for pharmaceuticals and fertilizers and higher-priority uses. Less exposed wall space in a smaller townhouse or row house which shares structural components with its neighbors leaves more energy to invest in a merry-go-round in the adjoining park.

All the changes in the human environment, with emphasis on the individual and the neighborhood, will also add to the attractiveness of the middle-sized and smaller cities. Santa Fe, New Mexico, for example, has made an effort to slow its growth and has avoided the unfortunate environmental destruction that has marred cities and vast areas of the countryside in such fast-growing states as California, Florida, Arizona and Colorado.

In an era when the skylines of Denver, Houston, Phoenix, Atlanta and Minneapolis all have a similar look, the adobe structures of Santa Fe stand out like a desert oasis. The reason Santa Fe is a singular, resplendent city today is that it stubbornly refused to grow as other U.S. urban areas grew. Unlike Albuquerque, Tucson, El Paso and other southwestern cities, Santa Fe did not throw away its Spanish-Indian heritage. Rather, Santa Fe retained it and developed a unique, colorful blend of lifestyles all its own. The Santa Fe Chamber of Commerce has never mounted a campaign for more industries and the city has no big, offensive, grimy factories.

This restraint has reduced the city's affluence— jobs have never been plentiful and per capita incomes are below the national average. But such indices are no better than population trends as guides to the quality of life. Santa Fe has tranquil living and people who savor it. It is one of the few major cities that has not based its planning on extravagant population trend projections or strained its resources trying to make these projections come true.

It is also one of the few U.S. cities that steadfastly refused to allow the construction of skyscrapers. The city has preserved the Spanish-Pueblo style of architecture and character that made it an artists' colony a half century ago. Being the geographic center of the Pueblo Indian civilization, surrounded by rugged national forests and parks, and overflowing with history, Santa Fe had the advantage of starting off well endowed. Other communities, however, have started with as much and sold their heritage for the stale porridge of progress.

More compact, better designed cities, neighborhoods and individual homes or apartments can go far to help us achieve the energy belt-tightening which must be achieved if we are to cope with the energy crisis. In this instance conservation and good design go in tandem.

There are several ways to enable existing housing to get better use of energy. With 27 million houses in the nation estimated to have little or no insulation, rising fuel costs and diminishing supplies make it necessary that new standards of home insulation, and financial assistance to induce such improvements, be established. The insulation can produce significant savings in fuel bills for the homeowner. With half a foot of insulation in the ceiling and a quarter foot in the walls, a well-insulated house would be approximately 60 percent more efficient. If the average cost of this level of insulation is an additional $200 for the medium-size house, and an inadequately protected home has an annual fuel bill of $400, the increased efficiency would only have to be 50 percent to recoup the investment in insulation over the first year.

The careful planting of trees and shrubs, the use of special double-pane windows, and the purchase of better appliances can also result in significant fuel savings. Major appliances, like air conditioners, for example, can require much more electricity to do the same cooling job. Frost-free refrigerators use half again as much energy as the standard models. Baths and hot-water laundering make greater demands on the water heater than showers and the use of cold-water detergents. The list ranges from gas stove pilot lights burning twenty-four hours a day to instant-on color television sets.

The key for all consumers is to demand durable, efficient appliances and require that all household appliances carry a label telling how much electricity or gas they use in performing their intended functions. In this way energy efficiency can become part of the competitive business system and save consumers money.

New architecture must demand that buildings be designed for multiple use and be integral, supportive elements in the life of a community. This kind of design, which values, plans and builds upon the neighborhood concept, will also further energy conservation.

In many existing buildings, a reasonably successful energy conservation program can begin with nothing more than a conscious effort to promote efficiency. While more extensive retrofitting of these buildings with better mechanical equipment and selective controls can achieve large, long-lasting improvements in energy use, some surprising savings can be achieved through simple housekeeping measures such as cutting out excessive lighting, tuning heating and air-conditioning systems more finely, lowering thermostats in the winter and raising them in the summer, and paying greater attention to maintenance.

In a nationwide demonstration of simple housekeeping techniques, the supervisory agency for some ten thousand federal government office buildings across the country (the General Services Administration) was able to save nearly a million barrels of crude oil in the first eight months of an energy conservation program initiated in July 1973 by removing 1.2 million fluorescent light tubes, setting the thermostats at 65 to 68 degrees in the winter and 76 to 78 degrees in the summer and reducing the use of autos. GSA buildings and cars operated with nearly 20 percent less fuel during the final quarter of 1973, in comparison with the same period the previous year.

For new buildings, more efficient use of energy involves more than lowering the heat and the air conditioner and turning out the lights. By careful planning and design, energy use can be cut at least in half in the new generation of buildings. No factor in energy conservation is more important than comprehensive planning before a structure is translated into concrete, steel and glass. Just as a building is given a dollar budget, so too it should have an energy budget to encourage consideration of how all aspects of the various fuel-eating systems of a structure integrate—so that heating, lighting, cooling, ventilation and other systems complement each other from the beginning.

When cheap energy in architecture could be taken for granted, new buildings took on a cookie-cutter sameness of design, changed only by outside ornamentation. By eliminating the outside environment in favor of a mechanically controlled inner climate, it did not matter whether a building was in Phoenix or in Philadelphia, as the style repeated itself in city after city. In learning to take advantage of the natural environment and be more responsive to the human dimension, architects and engineers will be developing new building types which utilize regional climatic characteristics to create a diversity of styles, structures and appearances suited to local conditions and building materials.

New building design must also learn to use the sun as a welcome partner. In its most uncomplicated form, this means using solar heat in the winter, rejecting or using it to run cooling machinery in the summer, and taking advantage of natural lighting whenever possible. So, too, natural winds and breezes must be used to good advantage.

Sealed glass buildings cannot take advantage of natural ventilation and must compensate for excessive solar heating in the summer and loss of heat in the winter. These conditions place an extra burden on the artificial heating and cooling systems. More effective building design will make discriminating use of glass to let in heat and light where desired, and, with the careful placement of the building, its shape and orientation will be designed for the best exposure to the sun and wind.

The potential for energy savings in building design is immense. Some examples are so obvious they have been ignored. In present office buildings, as much as 50 percent of the energy used to operate the structure goes for lighting. At least half of this lighting is excessive and misused. A greater flexibility in selective lighting and switching systems offers a very reasonable alternative to the present practice of lighting entire ceilings when lighting is needed for only a small area.

Not only is the excessive use of artificial light foolish and wasteful where natural light can do the job just as well, every two units of energy wasted in unneeded artificial light adds to the heating load and must be removed by another unit of energy to operate the air conditioning system.

Good new design can use already-existing design methods and technology to take advantage of the illumination of natural light from the sun without heat gain by making discrete use of shading, setbacks, awnings, fins, eyebrows and other architectural devices to selectively screen windows or glass areas during certain periods of the day from the glaring rays of the sun. New forms of insulated windows prevent heat loss or gain, and reflective types of glass have been developed to block a selected percentage of solar heat from adding to the building's cooling requirements while still providing illumination and good vistas.

Windows that can open also take advantage of natural ventilation. While there are 8,760 hours in every year, most buildings are used for some 3,000 hours. In New York City, it has been estimated that for at least one-sixth of these hours a building could be ventilated solely by outside air, if there were windows that could be opened to take advantage of fresh air.

Trees, shrubs and similar greenery also provide natural air conditioners to protect buildings. In the spring and summer they block the rays of the sun and offer shade to exposed outer surfaces. Photosynthesis freshens the air by absorbing carbon dioxide and giving off oxygen, cooling the breezes through the evaporation of moisture. Then in the fall, when the warming rays of the sun are welcome, there is a natural thermostat which sheds the leafy cover in a colorful display which man cannot duplicate by turning a switch.

The heating and cooling systems of large buildings can also be substantially improved. At present many buildings use large chilling units to cool all the incoming air supply and then reheat the same air to heat the building. Building in better equipment designed to operate at maximum efficiency when and where needed will also require attention to utilization and recovery of waste heat from refrigeration units and other exhaust systems. It will mean the increased use of the heat pump, essentially an air conditioner in reverse. Electric heat pumps can operate at the same output with as little as one-quarter the energy as is required by conventional electric heating and cooling methods.

The search to make maximum use of otherwise wasted heat will lead to an increase in "total energy" systems. Total energy systems require a sufficient population density and a commercial center that pulses with activity on a twenty-four-hour basis, or a neighborhood which has multiple functions throughout the day and generates its own electricity from burning fossil fuel. They capture the waste heat from the generation process and use it for space heating, air conditioning and hot water. In more sophisticated total energy systems, sewage and solid-waste conversion processes are also used. Such total energy systems serve the residential, commercial and industrial sectors of the community with two or three times the efficiency that is obtained if electricity is generated outside in conventional fashion. Depending on a variety of factors, such energy systems can be operated on smaller scales, such as in buildings or on the neighborhood level.

New attitudes which create an environment that understands human needs and rejects waste will also put height limitations on new buildings. At some point as the floors pile higher and higher there is a diminishing return on the advantages that density gives in the use of energy. More energy is needed for the mechanical support systems—elevators, ventilation ducts and pipelines, pumping of water, heat and cooled air. Large buildings also place intolerable burdens on mass transit facilities, water and sewage systems, solid waste disposal, streets, parks, and cultural facilities. Finally, they strangle wide areas of the community.

It is in the attitudes of citizens, both individually and collectively, that the prospect for acceptance of energy conservation rests. The necessary changes involve a fundamental reordering in the manner in which the public regards its lifestyles and surroundings. If the public understands these changes and demands such a reformation, then governments will have a mandate to legislate appropriate energy conservation standards, architects will be forced to design structures which complement neighborhoods and husband energy with jealous regard for waste, and manufacturers will be required to make the breakthroughs in introducing more durable, efficient products.

That citizens whose attitudes and values have changed are demanding new urbanization policies in this country is undeniable. The political impact of the nongrowth movement in the past five years is a case in point. A nongrowth stance by a state or city, which would have been regarded as unthinkable— if not downright un-American—a few years ago is already respectable.

The nongrowth movement is essentially an anti-sprawl movement, and is both a protest against the excessive costs imposed on taxpayers by ill-planned expansion and an expression of a desire of communities to guide or defer growth which would otherwise despoil existing environments. Although most leaders are still groping and have yet to articulate the specific policies needed to make nongrowth or managed growth work, such states as Hawaii, Oregon and Vermont have passed laws or enunciated plans which reflect a strong anti-growth perspective. To date the movement has included efforts to fix growth ceilings keyed to carrying capacities by putting a moratorium on the issuance of building permits or the approval of new sewer lines or subdivision plans. This has taken place in such endangered areas as the Lake Tahoe basin and Martha's Vineyard, and in such cities as Livermore, California, and Aspen, Colorado; and such counties as Loudon County, Virginia; Dade County, Florida; and Marin County, California.

This emphasis on a more realistic examination of growth comes with the increasing awareness of the hidden costs of continued expansion—costs that have been ignored for the past thirty years. Many people are now beginning to realize that along with the immediate economic gains from land purchases, job creation and the construction of new facilities come big increases in the public costs of schools, roads, water-treatment facilities and sewage and public safety services.

Particularly in those states and areas where it has been most pronounced, an awareness of the negative side of growth is readily apparent. It is no accident that slow-growth forces have gained strength in and at the edge of places like Denver, Colorado; Miami, Florida; San Diego and San Francisco, California; and Long Island, New York, where populations have doubled, trebled and even quadrupled since the 1950s, and angry citizens are opposing the rapacious development which destroys their environments and increases their taxes.

Boulder, Colorado, a city of 73,000 people which has seen its population increase over 80 percent since 1960, provides a particularly interesting case study of the impact of nongrowth attitudes. Described by civic leaders as the "nicest town in America," the growth issue came to a head in 1970, when the Boulder Valley Comprehensive Plan was adopted by the city and county. It predicted that population in the 58-square-mile county would double again in twenty years to 140,000. A survey was conducted and found that more than 70 percent of the residents wanted to retard further growth and stabilize Boulder's population around 100,000.

An amendment establishing such a population limitation was defeated on the November 1971 ballot, but 70 percent of the voters did support a resolution directing the government to "take all steps necessary to hold the rate of growth in the Boulder Valley to a level substantially below that experienced in the 1960s" and to conduct a study to recommend an optimum size for the city.

The innovative citizens of Boulder also won a city charter amendment establishing a maximum height of 55 feet for new buildings in dense areas of the community and 35 feet for low-density, residential areas, and defeated a proposal for a regional shopping center.

Although critics have argued that nongrowth policies are exclusionary, can cause unemployment in the construction industry, and will inevitably discriminate against the poor, it is likely that this new movement will continue to gain strength. The truth is that the *old* housing and urban growth policies were exclusionary, caused wild fluctuations in employment in the building trades, and discriminated against the poor. Once the nongrowth movement is correctly perceived as a push for compact communities and an end to wasteful sprawl, it will, we predict, gain wide acceptance in this country. Creative growth alternatives are desperately needed in an energy-short country which has spread itself too thin across the land. The movement toward growth guidance may represent a constructive turning point in U.S. urbanization if it produces well-designed cluster housing and neighborhood amenities which accommodate the needs of a cross-section of our society.

It takes no sudden surge of positive thinking to make us realize that energy shortages and the new design ideas discussed in this chapter offer an opportunity to improve life in this country. The environment—now substantially urban and suburban—is ugly, chaotic and dangerous to life and health. Much of what we have built is now either slum or potential slum, and it is sadly absurd that the world's richest nation has some of the most unsatisfying environments.

A highly mobile nation is almost by definition a rootless nation, without either a sense of place or a sense of community. The structural reforms we must carry out offer us a chance to redo our whole environment—a chance to gain control over our lives and make our lifestyles more humanizing. As we undertake the exciting tasks which lie ahead, we will perceive that the age of automania and cheap oil was really an age of escapism, a turning away from the institutions and personal values that are most lifegiving in the long run. In the process we may learn that the real answer to the "law and order" problem which is stifling this country lies in building neighborhoods and cities which have a sense of place and restoring the mutual sympathy between human beings which is the ultimate source of civilization. Jane Jacobs put the whole issue of personal security in its proper context when she wrote a decade ago:

> The public peace—the sidewalk and street peace—is not kept primarily by the police, necessary as the police are. It is kept primarily by an intricate, almost unconscious, network of voluntary controls and standards among the people themselves, and enforced by the people themselves. . . . No amount of police can enforce civilization where the normal, casual enforcement of it has broken down.

Better cities and better neighborhoods mean better neighbors. It is as simple as that. When people live at a slower pace and are closer to the earth and closer to other people we will begin to evolve the richer lifestyles for which many Americans yearn.

chapter eight

THE INDUSTRIAL
REFORMATION

"We're going to have to learn more about how to use
less better."

—Robert P. Neuschel
International Management Consultant
1974

For a go-lean strategy to succeed in a period of
scarcities, the most important reorientation must
occur in the industrial sector, where the biggest
users and biggest wasters of energy are situated.
More than 40 percent of all U.S. energy is consumed
by industry. Unless rigorous belt-tightening occurs
in board rooms where low-cost energy has long been
a minor item in corporate accounting, no national
program of conservation will be effective.

It will take a major effort to reorient the captains
of big industry. Their adherence to the bigger-is-
better ideology runs deep, and, until recently they
assumed cheap power would always be available.
Moreover, their economists usually assured them few
economies could be achieved by investing capital in
energy-saving efforts.

Big industry's response to a wide-ranging study, "The Potential for Energy Conservation," made in 1972 by the Office of Emergency Preparedness in the White House, was quite predictable. The report concluded that it was possible to reduce the demand for energy by 1980 by the equivalent of 7.3 million barrels of oil every day. Put another way, the total energy savings projected in the OEP study would be considerably more than the flow of three Alaskan pipelines. More than one-third of that potential savings would result from the introduction of more efficient processes and equipment into the industrial sector. But industry's response to this public discovery of an "Alaskan" pipeline in its own back yard was hardly enthusiastic. The initial reaction was that, given the low level of present fuel prices, industry was burning up energy supplies as efficiently as possible.

This dogmatic position was foreseeable. American industry is characterized by an all-out commitment to "economies of scale"—which means an aggressive commitment to automation, to big technology, and to ever-bigger plants. Such a wanton approach to industrial power escaped close scrutiny until the Arab embargo put a spotlight on wasteful practices.

Of course, signs of the profligate use of energy in U.S. manufacturing were cropping up well before the recent embargo. All through the twentieth century, great claims have been made about the productivity of American industry—more and more goods for each hour of labor, and, with increasing automation, more dollars of production for each unit of energy. From 1920 until 1960, improvements in productivity steadily reduced the amount of energy needed for each dollar of GNP from over 140,000 BTUs to fewer than 93,000 BTUs. Further advances brought the energy cost for every dollar of production down another 6,000 BTUs by 1965. At that point, however, our vaunted efficiency and improved productivity began to deteriorate. Whereas it took about 87,000 BTUs to churn out another dollar's worth of goods and get them into the consumer's hands in 1965, by 1970 the energy input for each dollar's worth of goods had climbed back to 95,000 BTUs, the level of the mid-1950s.

As we have found in other areas of energy use, there are important short-term conservation steps which can be taken. In industry, many such measures involve what might be called housekeeping, the kind of efficiency engineering which seeks to stretch the fuel used to run existing machines to provide light, heat, and process steam for plant operations. Some of this housekeeping, though of the most elemental sort, has not been pursued because energy conservation was not in the vocabulary of industrial management until very recently. Yet leaking pipes and valves, processed heat vented through the smokestack, mistuned boilers, uninsulated furnaces and transmission lines, and idle machinery all add significantly to industrial energy waste.

Long-term reforms have much greater potential, and are more dramatic. They involve nothing less than a radical rethinking of the aims and methods of our whole industrial system. Evidence is piling up that enormous energy savings are possible if many promising new concepts are pursued. These reforms, however, involve drastic changes in the kinds of goods we manufacture, the amount of virgin raw materials we use, and the very size and scale of the U.S. industrial establishment.

The Short-Term Measures

A few resourceful companies have already demonstrated what can be accomplished in the short run through the application of commonsense conservation engineering. Significant economies can be achieved through such simple measures as the use of heat pumps, reductions in the use of light, and extra investments to make machines and processes perform at higher levels of efficiency.

Once the concept of energy conservation is accepted as corporate policy, the payoffs can be surprising. For example, Raytheon, the big East Coast electronics company, cut its fuel bill an astonishing 30 percent by efficiency engineering; and California's Lockheed Aircraft Company achieved a 23 percent reduction through different housekeeping measures. However, the most forceful example of energy-frugal engineering is the record set by the giant E. I. Du Pont Company in the past seven years. Since Du Pont, a heavy user of electricity and other forms of energy, started their efficiency program, total energy use has increased only about 10 percent during a period when plant output was increasing more than 50 percent. Du Pont's energy experts not only cut consumption in its old plants, but they gained support for major capital investments in highly efficient new plants, processes and machines. With few exceptions, U.S. industry has operated on the theory that it was sound for initial capital investments to be as low as possible. Du Pont explicitly rejected this premise, and, at a time when fuel costs are skyrocketing, their extra capital outlays will be repaid many times over as they recover the total capital and operating costs over the full cycle of their plant and equipment.

For some companies, finding new ways to save energy is not only prompted by the pocketbook promise of a lower fuel bill; natural gas and petroleum are also crucial as the raw materials for their products. This predicament led the Celanese Company's energy conservation task force to identify 265 energy feedstock savings projects in their various operations. Although these projects would cost the company upwards of $23 million to implement, the potential savings in fuel and raw materials would amount to $35 million.

The real short-term energy savings can be obtained by introducing known updated processes and equipment into just five industries: steel, aluminum, petroleum, cement and paper. These five are the biggest industrial energy sponges in the country and use up close to half of the industrial energy and about 16 percent of all the energy consumed in the United States each year. Here, the application of existing technology could have a large impact, if industrial managers and financiers have the foresight to recognize the value of energy conservation. If the cement industry, for example, used known waste-saving techniques and applied processes being installed in Europe, 60 percent of the energy presently used to produce one ton of cement could be saved. With a conservation potential of this magnitude, the cement industry could continue to increase its rate of production each year through 1980 and end up consuming less total fuel than it did in 1968.

The aluminum industry is another area where new attitudes produce big changes. Aluminum companies use enormous quantities of electricity. For many years they had all the low-cost, leftover power they needed in the TVA area and in the Pacific Northwest. However, sensing that power shortages would force big price increases in the 1970s, ALCOA made a concentrated research effort to perfect a more efficient process for converting bauxite into aluminum. The result was a new technology that will reduce the power needed to produce a pound of aluminum in this energy-intensive industry by nearly one-third.

In one sense, industries have been fuel-gluttons because we had an energy system that encouraged overuse. It is predictable that rising energy costs and shortages will impel energy efficiency and encouarge other companies to copy the reforms pioneered by Du Pont and ALCOA and others. In the past, government policies and the use-more-pay-less promotional plans of utility companies subsidized the lavish use of energy by fostering bulk power contracts which persuaded executives and plant managers that their fuel bills would always be minor items. With the waning of the petroleum age, however, such waste-encouraging arrangements are outmoded, and as the big users face new inverted rate schedules (which constitute an imperative reform) and much higher power bills, we may expect to see creative industrial engineers produce a whole new range of startling efficiency innovations.

The Long-Range Reforms

Admittedly, Americans are still too cocksure about their success formulas to be open-minded about drastic energy reforms which would change the size and scope of the U.S. industrial establishment. Most of us are still convinced that the year 2000 will see twice as much production and consumption of almost everything, and most of us still hold to the belief that scientists will come up with a cheap substitute for oil.

We are in trouble today because the American experience has been based upon expansion and growth. We still cling to the creed of unlimited expansion and congratulate ourselves for building nearly everything bigger. We continue to seek out and design faster machines. From paper towels and beverage containers to snowmobile production, U.S. industry follows a pattern of ever-redoubling growth.

In such a climate of consensus it is considered heretical for industrial leaders to contemplate any scaling down of their plans or to reassess cherished national goals. Today most industrialists cannot envision an economic system that is leaner, or needs less energy per capita. To a conventional industrialist, "less" is equated with business stagnation and failure. It is somehow perceived as a threat to the American way of life. For example, electric power executives accept as an article of faith that the consumption of electricity will continue to double every decade. Steelmen and the producers of the other primary metals similarly foresee vast increases in requirements for their products. The economists, eyes glued to their holy grail of GNP, ominously predict that a slackening of growth in our basic industries would mean that millions would be thrown out of work, that the poor would remain poor, and the rich would lose some of their luxuries.

At the moment we remain a nation of megathinkers: more-is-always-better is the guiding thought. However, it is now an obstacle to real progress and should be recognized as an icon of another era. We cannot concentrate on major industrial reforms so long as we are misled by grandiose illusions about our future that are based on tarnished principles of the past. The extraordinary addiction of many industrialists to cherished corporate notions of projected production levels was illustrated in 1974 when Richard Gerstenberg of General Motors gave his stockholders a pep-talk on the impact of present energy shortages on GM. All that the "short-term" energy problem meant, Gerstenberg explained, was that the United States would have a "14-million-car year" in the early 1980s rather than in 1978.

Such an attitude reflects a conglomerate mind-set that focuses solely upon gains in production and consumption—sales volume advances—as the way to increase returns on capital investments in public-owned corporations. So long as energy remained a constant factor in production, abundant in supply and inexpensive (in fact, becoming cheaper the more that it was used), corporate managers could concentrate on mechanizing and multiplying production to widen profit margins on each unit and to pile up overall earnings.

Given this state of mind, it is obvious that broad structural reforms will not be carried out until intractable shortages force us to recognize that we are entering a new era in which there will probably be less energy per capita, not more. There should be no self-deception on this point: the structural reforms in our industrial system which should be part of a new national agenda will probably not come about as a result of industrial statesmanship or enlightened self-interest. Some of them will be forced upon industry by escalating energy costs which cannot be automatically absorbed in production without a reduction in profit margin per unit or passed on to the customer without a drop in sales volume. Others will be an outgrowth of severe shortages of raw materials which put a ceiling upon production. Changes will occur only when the laws of economics and the laws enacted by governments combine to make full-scale resource recovery and recycling a reality; and still other reforms will gain acceptance as industrialists realize that sound conservation enhances, and does not undermine, profits.

Few have noticed it, but the pinches we have felt the past year already initiated this chain of events. Energy is no longer cheap and abundant. Virgin raw materials are becoming scarcer each day. These shortages are beginning to dictate some actions. For one thing, there is a movement toward smaller cars, buildings and machines. The same shortages, we believe, will also induce a trend toward durable, long-lasting goods; an end to planned obsolescence manufacturing; the beginning of a systematic recycling of all resources; and a shift from the production of goods to the providing of services.

The Economies of Scaling Down

The size and bulk of American automobiles have steadily increased since the time of the first Model-T Ford. The building of record-size skyscrapers has been a constant contest of corporate clients, architects and builders since the invention of the elevator. From here on, shortages of materials and rising costs, as well as the necessity for operating efficiencies, will relentlessly scale down the size of such machines and projects. This development should be as welcome as it is inevitable. In addition to the extravagant amounts of energy needed to operate the leviathan luxury cars and egregious examples of egocentric architecture, the manufacturing process itself consumes tremendous amounts of materials and energy. In turn these processes make enormous demands on supplier industries which are themselves big energy consumers. These are the very industries which must lead the way if there is to be a major energy conservation breakthrough.

A handful of energy-intensive industries—the primary metals such as steel, aluminum, copper and zinc; cement; chemicals; as well as the petroleum industry itself—consumes close to 75 percent of the total energy used by U.S. industry. It is therefore fortuitous that an across-the-board scale-down of size will simultaneously scale down the energy and raw material needs of these king-size industrial consumers.

The bellwether industry of America, automobiles, is a prime example of the potential for resource conservation. The automobile is an assembled amalgam of raw materials and finished products, many of them imported, which range from natural rubber and plastics to chrome and steel. More than any other artifact of our society, the American luxury car symbolizes our belief that bigger is better, heavier is safer, and more speed is devoutly to be desired. How ironic that the "family-size" car has been getting larger and heavier over the past fifteen years while the average U.S. family has been declining to its smallest size in history!

Hindsight already tells us that the dream of the automakers of ever-bigger cars and ever-larger annual sales ad infinitum was one of the grand illusions of the Petroleum Age. This illusion persists today, even though all indicators suggest that the trend toward mini-cars is irreversible. The myth of ever-increasing auto expansion could not be punctured so long as there was a glut of cheap gasoline at the pump and an abundance of cheap oil to enable the supplier industries to mine and manufacture their products. Now that such favorable conditions no longer exist, the urgent reshaping of this industry can produce potentially enormous savings of energy.

We are convinced that if America makes a determined effort to stretch its petroleum supplies, the auto industry will be forced to produce cars within this decade which weigh 60 percent less than today's behemoths. The gasoline situation itself should force upon customers, and finally upon automakers, the realization that miles-per-gallon are directly related to weight; a 5,000-pound automobile consumes 100 percent more gas than a 2,500-pound car with the same equipment. This one step will have a massive domino effect on the energy-intensive companies that supply the products which comprise a car. And the impact will be heightened further if, as seems likely, the total U.S. auto population slowly shrinks and transportation modes become more diverse.

Such a scale-down could well lead the historic turnaround in energy conservation. If the average car weighs 60 percent less and the diet is apportioned evenly, this means that a car will contain roughly 60 percent fewer basic materials and so forth. Of course, such a reduction in the demand for these products will proportionately lower the energy needs of the supplier industries. To "go small" means a shrinkage throughout the process.

There are indications that Detroit may make such changes willingly. In 1974 an American Motors executive viewed small cars as "a permanent rather than temporary response" to the energy crisis because of increasing resource shortages. It is energy and resource shortages that will dictate the pace of change. There is no way either Detroit, or its suppliers, or Washington can keep the production spiral going in a new period of waning petroleum and material supplies.

The construction of commerical office buildings is another example where the scaling down of materials used offers another major opportunity for energy savings. Recent detailed studies have demonstrated that the amount of steel, reinforced concrete and other materials used in most office buildings is much greater that what is needed for safety and sound design. This is yet another area where plentiful energy and resources invited excesses. Most safety standards in city building codes (which prescribe the amounts of structural steel and reinforced concrete needed in a specific building) were formulated during our cheap energy years, and they treat direct and indirect energy costs as an insignificant item. However, the best engineering techniques of today have proven that more frugal construction practices could reduce the materials used in future large office buildings by as much as 50 percent without sacrificing safety. Here again is a potential for big reductions in the consumption of raw materials and the energy used in their industrial conversion.

We are convinced that the age of megastructures and elephantine construction schemes has been doomed by the resource shortages which lie ahead. Rising costs and shortages will force clients, architects and builders to compress or abandon their remaining grandiose plans. A return to modest-sized apartments, commercial centers and office buildings is indicated on every count. Energy-squandering high-rise buildings must give way to energy-saving low-rise structures, and multifamily cluster housing must again become commonplace in this country. It is entirely likely that by 1990 few buildings will be built any higher than their surrounding trees.

As this scaling-down process gains momentum, our engineers may finally begin to take Buckminster Fuller's concept of "ephemeralization" seriously, and begin to understand the virtue and the process of doing more with less. Fuller may be one of the honored prophets of the new age of scarcity. He has repeatedly challenged his profession to use efficiency engineering to solve problems, but up to now he has been treated as an impractical romantic. Fuller's work, the antithesis of the big-engineering approach, is filled with a whole range of less-is-more proposals suitable for a time of shortages. He illustrates his main thesis, for example, by pointing out that a Telstar satellite weighing only one-tenth of a ton can out-perform 75,000 tons of trans-Atlantic cable. It is already foreseeable that once such creative engineering concepts come of age, radical ideas and concepts depicted as "exotic" or unfeasible will soon become a driving force in conventional engineering.

The Return to Durable Products

The abandonment of planned obsolescence manufacturing in favor of the creation of durable products is yet another fundamental alteration in industrial lifestyle that would produce large energy savings.

Fifty years ago, durability was the sine qua non of U.S. manufacturing. Razors, watches, clocks and many other products were literally made to "last a lifetime." In those days, frugal people wanted long-lived machines and products which were simple enough that they could be maintained in good operating condition. Inventors and engineers put durability first in their designs, and everything from the Model-A Ford to household appliances exemplified a commitment by manufacturers to the production of serviceable, long-lasting goods.

Understandably, the idea of planned obsolescence manufacturing became feasible only when the Petroleum Age came to a full flower. The automobile industry was again the father of a wasteful concept, and high-pressure advertising was its skillful midwife. Alfred P. Sloan's annual "model change" got planned

obsolescence launched in the 1930s. It took postwar
affluence and subliminal advertising, however, to
make it a dominant force in the U.S. industrial system. A shameless, ruthless campaign undermined the
idea of thrift, whetted our acquisitive impulses and
subtly changed our social ethics and our personal
values. Eric Larrabee, the social critic, put the mind-
changing technique in perspective in the late 1950s
when he wrote:

> In Detroit the equations are fixed: small equals cheap
> equals bad, and large equals expensive equals good.
> Detroit has no way of appealing to the small-car cus-
> tomer without insulting him; it offers him the tail
> end of the procession, and never lets him forget it.

Even the much-vaunted American Puritan ethic
could not withstand the transposing of basic values
which was imbedded in this subversive concept. It
displaced thrift with one-upmanship and people were
urged to surpass the Joneses, not merely keep up
with them. It gave everyone a vested interest in slip-
shod products and patterns of prodigal consumption.

As "discretionary" incomes expanded after World
War II, the energy feast turned into an orgy. With
the years of restraint compelled by a depression and
a war finally over, it was easy to persuade gullible
souls that "new" or flashier or bigger things were
better. Soon, the planned obsolescence concept in-
fected the whole manufacturing sector. The producers of razor blades, refrigerators, radios joined in,
and the hectic process of turning over huge quantities

of short-lived, shoddy goods made even the old-timers forget the virtues of durable products. To make things worse, the container industry pitched in and enlarged the concept by inventing throwaway cans, bottles, and packages that promised convenience at the expense of conservation.

In retrospect, the consumer society we created was largely a stepchild of planned obsolescence production. The latter altered our values and our concept of ourselves. Writing in the late 1950s, Victor Lebow pungently described the changeover:

> Our enormously productive economy . . . demands that we make consumption our way of life, that we convert the buying and use of goods into rituals, that we seek our spiritual satisfactions, our ego satisfactions, in consumption. . . . We need things consumed, burned up, worn out, replaced, and discarded at an ever-increasing rate.

The energy crisis and the growing shortage of cheap virgin raw materials has now made the concept of planned obsolescence itself obsolete. We can no longer afford its false values and its inordinate demands on our resources. The throwaway lifestyle was always an absurdity—a hothouse flower of the brief age of cheap energy. We must change our ways of production and emphasize consumer goods that are easy to repair and built to last. This should be a welcome challenge and rewarding task for our jaded production experts. The American people, when confronted by necessity, have always excelled at ingenious inventions and the production of serviceable goods.

Whether one contemplates cars, gadgets, or home appliances, there is no doubt that a switch to the manufacturing of durable products can be achieved. It is a calumny on American ingenuity to suggest otherwise. The protectors of the industrial status quo are guilty of many outrages against their consumers for failing to bring more durable goods onto the markets. It was a scandal in 1973, for instance, when Porsche displayed a car designed to have a twenty-year life (or to travel at least 200,000 miles) at an international auto show in Europe, but quickly assured its fellow manufacturers that it had no intention of mass producing such a long-lived vehicle.

There is no precise way to calculate the energy and resources which can be saved by a return to a durable goods economy. However, a rough rule of thumb tells us that, if we make goods that last two or three times as long, then two or three times less energy and resources will be required in each industry affected.

The most far-reaching change in our industrial system will come with the advent of what some scientists are already referring to as a "recycling society." Conservation will then become an integral part of our way of life. It is noteworthy that Dr. Glenn T. Seaborg, the former chairman of the Atomic Energy Commission who in the past was invariably an optimistic advocate of big-technology solutions, has predicted recently that in the next twenty years the U.S. will be forced to institute a complete regimen for recycling our resources. In Seaborg's recycling society, ". . . the present material situation is literally reversed: all waste and scrap—what are now called 'secondary materials'—become our major resources and our natural, untapped resources become our backup supplies."

However, the recycling society we must build will involve far more than the reuse of "secondary materials." It will mean the conversion of our energy-rich garbage and sewage for fuel. It will also mean the use of animal wastes as valuable fertilizer or synthetic fuel, and an emphasis on organic agriculture as petroleum-based fertilizers become more scarce. It will mean that every industrial plant will find ways to reuse its own material and energy wastes (plants producing excess heat or process steam will either find uses for this by-product or convert it into electricity). Finally, it will mean that other states will follow Connecticut's example and build regional recycling centers to process all garbage and solid wastes generated by city dwellers and industries.

In 1973, Connecticut became the first state in the country to adopt a statewide plan for recycling wastes. Ten resource recovery plants are scheduled for construction throughout the state. By 1985, Connecticut will be recycling 60 percent of its industrial and household wastes for materials and energy, enough to provide over 10 percent of the state's electricity and enough scrap steel for the manufacture of 200,000 cars. The coming shortages of critical materials will make it both prudent and profitable to end the waste of "wastes" and reuse all of our resources.

With few exceptions, all virgin resources are recyclable or recoverable from our waste stream. Even metal alloys can be reused if we are sensible and tag or code them for recycling. Certain recoveries can be made before items enter the post-consumer waste stream and become mixed with garbage or otherwise contaminated. Thus, automobiles are a valuable source of segregated scrap metal, while newspapers and corrugated paper deserve separate collection for the reuse of their fibers. Old buildings are also valued for their scrap steel, and, depending upon their scrap content, wrecking companies seek such buildings and offer free demolition.

Increasingly, the municipal trashpile is recognized as a minerals storehouse. The Environmental Protection Agency estimates that over half the iron, aluminum, copper, lead and tin in the municipal waste stream of the United States could be recovered. These materials could provide 7 percent of the iron, 8 percent of the aluminum, 20 percent of the tin, and 3 percent of the lead that is consumed in this country each year. For two of these metals, this level of recovery from the waste stream is particularly important. Today, more than 90 percent of the bauxite used in aluminum production comes from foreign sources and virtually all of the tin used in this country is imported.

Evidence is already at hand which indicates that energy savings would be enormous if a full-scale conversion were made to resource recovery. Predictably, the biggest payoff of all will come in highly intensive primary metal and paper industries. For example, recycled steel requires 75 percent less energy than steel made from iron ore; 70 percent less energy is used in recycling paper than in using virgin pulp; and twelve times as much energy is needed to produce primary aluminum as to recover aluminum scrap.

Further energy savings can be achieved by utilizing the 80 percent of consumer trash that is combustible as a fossil fuel substitute or as the raw hydrocarbons to synthesize gas or oil. The energy that is retrievable from the municipal trash heap could supply up to 2 percent of our current national demand, or the equivalent of nearly 700,000 barrels of oil a day.

In addition to the energy and resource savings that can be achieved through the recycling of metals and other materials from the trash and the utilization of the combustible organic fraction of the waste stream for direct burning or synthetic fuel processing, the recycling of wastes reduces the unnatural stresses upon the environment to an extraordinary degree. Through materials separation and combustion, solid waste is reduced by some 90 percent, and both air and water pollution is diminished. Secondary environmental benefits also accrue from the diminished demand for the processing of virgin materials, which requires such large amounts of energy.

There are big problems to be solved, however, if the pathway to nationwide recycling is to be cleared. It will take major new laws and drastic changes in tax policies to make recycling function as it should. All our laws must encourage the recycling process. Those who invest in resource recycling should receive our biggest tax benefits, just as we should revise all outmoded laws which encourage the rapid depletion of virgin resources.

Fortunately, recycling will give a much-needed second wind to the environmental movement as it brings environmental enhancement and resource conservation into the same harness. In 1972 the state of Oregon passed a pioneering law prohibiting the sale of nonreturnable bottles and cans. The plan has worked extremely well. With one bold stroke it has improved the environment, reduced reliance on virgin raw materials (an average bottle can be reused twenty-five or thirty times), and significantly decreased the amount of energy consumed by the container industry. This is a dramatic example of the benefits of the big turnaround. It has been roughly calculated that if all the states—or the Congress— were to pass similar laws, such statutes would save as much electricity each year as is used by the homeowners in Boston, Washington, Pittsburgh and San Francisco. In addition to saving about one-half of 1 percent of the nation's total energy bill and cleaning the environment of nonreturnable bottles, there would be a net gain in employment in the retail and distribution sector of the economy.

Although we believe that recycling is vital to America's future, most economists and industrialists fear that a significant slackening of energy consumption would do serious damage to the economy and result in increased rates of unemployment. Their view is that unless energy use continues to follow the postwar pattern of substantial annual increases, U.S. prosperity cannot be sustained. These experts point out that, despite some fluctuations, the amount of energy needed to produce one dollar of GNP is about the same now as it was in 1955, and they fear that if the rising energy consumption curve dips overall U.S. production is certain to decline also. Some even argue emotionally that our whole standard of living is at stake, and a rigorous conservation program would mean an ultimate return to "caves and candles." A nationally syndicated columnist expressed both the contempt and alarm of these spokesmen in 1971 when he wrote:

> We could reduce the necessity of converting fossil fuels into electrical energy by turning off our air conditioners, lighting beeswax candles, throwing out our refrigerators, TV and radio sets, and climbing more stairs. We could outlaw private cars and go back to bicycles. But we could not power our industries or maintain a transportation system with stove wood or charcoal, even if we could find the trees.

There is growing evidence that these energy standpatters are wrong. When one evaluates the economic achievements of the Japanese, for example, the 400-percent difference between their per capita energy use and ours clearly indicates that a go-lean U.S. strategy will not necessarily "wreck the economy" or foreclose further growth. The huge energy savings outlined in this book would entail major changes, to be sure, but the burden of proof should be on those who assert that such a gradual industrial reformation—emphasizing such things as a scaling down of engineering projects, the manufacture of durable goods and systematic resource recycling—would endanger the economy. The annual per capita energy consumption for industry and transportation in Great Britain is almost two-and-one-half times that of New Zealand, for example, yet the per capita GNPs of the two countries differ by less than 10 percent and few would argue that the quality of life in New Zealand is inferior to that in England.

Already, some U.S. economists are shifting ground on this crucial issue. An econometric computer study prepared by economists Dale Jorgenson and Edward Hudson of Data Resources, Inc., for the Ford Foundation's Energy Policy Project in 1974 forecasts only a tiny shrinkage in GNP by the year 2000 even if the energy growth rate is cut 50 percent. On the basis of their studies, these economists believe U.S. energy use soared in the past twenty years not because of need but because energy was so cheap and readily available. Jorgenson, a Harvard economist, scoffs at the conventional assumptions (an approach he calls "engineering thinking") and believes higher prices and other changes can curb energy demand without seriously damaging the economy. Hudson goes further and asserts flatly that "energy can be saved with little loss in GNP and without more unemployment." Such a doctrine represents a radical departure from past thinking about energy demand, but we predict a new consensus will form around it in the next few years as the potentials of energy conservation are demonstrated.

Events, of course, will decide who is right. If our analysis is even substantially correct, national prudence dictates at least some initial steps to move with the powerful winds of change that are blowing across the world landscape. We can elect to continue on our present head-long course and refuse to consider major changes in policies until a crash occurs, or we can begin a program of gradual adjustments now. As to the allegation that starting important turnaround adjustments now will inevitably mean unemployment and economic dislocations, we suggest that the risks of disruption are much larger and more inevitable if we resist change. If transitional steps are taken soon, there will be tens of thousands of new jobs in the new recycling and service industries. On the human side, if energy shortages eliminate some lavish forms of automation, employees will gain the satisfaction derived from practicing individual craftsmanship and small-grained skills in industries which increasingly value the person over the machine.

The developments we have described could also lead to a wise and long-overdue "division of labor" between nations. If the right political climate is developed, the large multinational corporations should play a creative global role by relocating many of the new energy-intensive industries in the oil-rich countries that want industrialization and are still burning off natural gas resources in the oil fields. Such an international sorting out of industrial functions would benefit everyone as the energy crunch intensifies.

Finally, from the national standpoint, a major industrial reformation is essential to strengthen our economy for the long haul. It is not in our national interest to continue the rapid depletion of our remaining petroleum reserves. The sooner we begin to close our own energy gap by go-lean measures that reduce waste, the sooner we will put our future on a sound footing.

With the global resource predicament becoming more intractable each year, the world desperately needs a conservation model as it enters the age of scarcity. The global overview is becoming crucial. We must learn to recycle and scale down our industrial appetites to human proportions. If we want to keep the respect of the world community in the years ahead, and if we seek to maintain the security that comes from reasonable self-sufficiency, we will have to go-lean and transform our outlook and our institutions.

chapter nine

THE FATEFUL DILEMMA: DOMESTIC CONSUMPTION AND GLOBAL SCARCITIES

"There are only 6 percent of the people of the world living in the United States, and we use 30 percent of all the energy. That isn't bad; that is good. That means we are the richest, strongest people in the world, and that we have the highest standard of living in the world. That is why we need so much energy, and may it always be that way."

—Richard M. Nixon
November 1973

"I believe it is highly questionable whether any country has a permanent right to a disproportionate share of the world's resources."

—Maurice Strong, Director,
United Nations Environment Program
November 1973

The human family is entering an ominous new phase of history. The global oil crisis alone has caused a massive, sudden shift in economic power—and interacting shortages of energy, food, and raw materials have already wiped out the hopes and plans of many nations for economic advancement. These events are creating tensions and moral dilemmas that will dominate the future: increasingly both the newly rich oil-producing nations and the traditionally superaffluent nations are perceived in a new light by their neighbors. As soon as events prove to the have-not countries that the new Age of Scarcity has doomed their expectations for betterment, a politics of desperation will displace the politics of hope, and poor people everywhere will suddenly see the world with new eyes and new anguish.

These tremors will also throw a relentless spotlight on the bloated U.S. economy and our luxurious lifestyle, and will produce many reappraisals and shifts of opinion. The poor nations, which comprise almost two-thirds of the inhabitants of Earth, will realize that the panaceas peddled by the rich nations have failed, and question the motives and lives of those who did the most to promote such nostrums.

As this change of outlook occurs, the United States will be far more vulnerable to criticism and blame than any other nation. We have been the leading prophet of salvation through science, the main advocate of the idea that economic growth is the answer to the world's problems and the principal propounder of the concept that there are enough resources for everyone. An ugly confrontation is certain. And our pretensions and promises most likely will be thrown back in our faces as the population-food crunch shatters nations and leaders of floundering countries focus angry attention on the extravagances and excesses of

U.S. society. Gluttony is a cardinal vice in a world running out of basic commodities. When the magnitude of our ravenous consumption of energy, food and raw materials is placed in context, President Nixon's statement that the U.S. will continue to use 30 percent of the planet's energy resources into the indefinite future may become as cruelly infamous as Marie Antoinette's capricious pronouncement to the starving citizens of France: "Let them eat cake!"

If we hope to maintain any semblance of world leadership in the Age of Scarcity, there is no leeway for such insensitive swagger by any prominent American—much less the President himself. The course is clear. This country cannot set itself up as the example for the world until it slackens its consumption of the world's resources. The frightful turn of events makes such continued profligacy irrational and untenable. Our thinking about the appropriate use of energy and material resources must be drastically altered in the next few years. For example, rich-nation growth, once universally regarded as a positive "good," will appear as self-centered greed; affluence, once widely admired, will be seen as gluttonous indifference; and the partial monopolization of energy or other resources, once viewed as an acceptable expedient by a great power country, will be perceived as a hostile act toward the world community.

It is terribly important that the American people quickly grasp the moral issues implicit in the energy crisis. Brutal events are daily emphasizing the interdependence of regions and nations and forcing world statesmen to discuss ways to share shortages and avoid bankrupting some nations. Although shaken by our Vietnam blunder, our leadership has been credible largely because most other nations believed we were a compassionate country which genuinely wanted to help other peoples improve their lot. This favorable image, however, can be erased overnight in a world of discredited ideas, empty stomachs and shrinking hopes. In a time of catastrophic shortages, a nation that owns half of the world's motor vehicles, eats one-third of its beef, and uses one-third of its raw materials cannot possibly maintain a reputation as a magnanimous "helper." If unbridled U.S. consumption continues, our claims to moral leadership will inevitably be forfeited.

Since 1945, Cold War expediency and American generosity have combined to produce the Marshall Plan, the Food for Peace Program, the Peace Corps and a whole range of useful foreign assistance programs. These efforts have imparted legitimacy to American world leadership. It has been the expressed willingness of this country to share its resources and its technical skills (a declaration of intentions that nearly always ran ahead of our performance, incidentally) that has won the respect, if not always the friendship, of the developing countries. This shrinking reservoir of good will, however, can be lost altogether unless we reorient our outlook and change our attitude toward the world's resources and the needs of other nations.

The best way to begin is to examine recent history

and to admit, with the benefit of hindsight, that we have committed some spectacular mistakes in the last three decades in trying to guide and assist the developing nations. The evidence at hand strongly suggests that at least three major errors were made. Each was based upon a fallacious assumption—an assumption central to our world view and our self-centered idea of our own economic aims.

The Technological Transformation Fallacy

The first fallacy was rooted in the faith that advanced technology alone would beneficently and conclusively transform the world, and that the best way for the wealthy, industrialized countries to help the poor nations develop was to export their technological expertise. This was not a unique U.S. idea, but we did far more to make it a central concept of nation building than other countries did. The "world of rising expectations" of the 1950s was an offspring of the Technological Transformation Fallacy. The cornucopian hypothesis it expressed was summed up in 1957 by an eminent group of U.S. scientists who wrote a book entitled *The Next Hundred Years:*

> If we are able in the decades ahead to avoid thermonuclear war, and if the present underdeveloped countries of the world are able to carry out successful industrialization programs, we shall approach the time when the world will be completely industrialized. And as we continue along this path we shall process ores of continually lower grade, until we finally shall sustain ourselves with materials obtained from the

rocks of the earth's crust, the gasses of the air, and the waters of the seas. By that time the mining industry as such will long since have disappeared and have been replaced by vast, integrated, multipurpose chemical plants supplied by rock, air and sea water from which will flow a multiplicity of products, ranging from fresh water to electric power, liquid fuels, and metals.

Buoyed by such superoptimism, technological sharing as a panacea for the world's problems became a central theme of U.S. foreign policy soon after World War II. Flushed with the success of the Marshall Plan in reconstructing the advanced economies of Western Europe and Japan, President Truman, in his inaugural address in 1949, made the glowing promise that the United States would "make available to peace-loving people the benefits of our store of technological knowledge in order to help them realize their aspirations for a better life." Americans assumed that such knowledge could work equally well for any nation. It became a basic premise of our foreign aid programs and gained new force when President Eisenhower unveiled the "Atoms for Peace" program in the mid-fifties with its glowing promise of low-cost, superabundant nuclear energy for all.

The Technological Transformation Fallacy inevitably led the U.S. into several mistakes. The first was the assumption that the developing countries would benefit readily from what might be called "big machine technology" and large-scale applications of science. The book *The Ugly American*, written in the late 1950s, was a critique of that part of the U.S. foreign aid program which drew upon this idea. Its authors pointed out that countries with subsistence economies needed simple machines, simple advances in agriculture, and such "crude" old-fashioned technologies as windmills and hand-powered water pumps far more than they needed bulldozers, cars or airports. In too many instances this nation was, figuratively, selling Cadillacs and combines to countries which had neither mechanics nor gas stations. It was this criticism, incidentally, which led to the establishment of the Peace Corps by President Kennedy with its emphasis on helping people help themselves by teaching such simple skills as building schools, developing supplies of potable water, and effecting elementary improvements in farming.

The second misjudgment concerned what the Technological Transformation Fallacy did to this country's conception of itself. In convincing itself that modest investments in "sharing technology" would produce long-range solutions for the poor countries, the United States was also reinforcing a belief that there was no inherent conflict between U.S. ambitions for escalating growth, which were already making inordinate demands on the world's supply of resources, and the fulfillment of the aspirations of the developing nations. The United States could, or so it was thought, have the best of both worlds: our technical/industrial experience could be passed on to assist the poor nations onto our path of development; at the same time, we could aggressively push our own explosive spiral of production and consumption.

The Superior Model Fallacy

The second fallacy was intertwined with hyperoptimism about technology. It also reflected the self-centered pride of Americans in the achievements of their society. If the quickest way to share progress and prosperity was by industrialization, it seemed logical to assume that the United States was a sound growth model for the "developing" countries—and to further assume that U.S. experience and technical skills could be readily transplanted abroad.

We are just beginning to realize that these assumptions were terribly misguided and led us into a major historical blunder. The U.S. was, and is, a country so atypical in its geography and in its man-land relationships that its history has always been singular. We live on a large continent—in the beneficent temperate zone—that contains a staggering storehouse of resources: soil, water, forests, petroleum, and minerals. Our supplies of these resources are so bountiful compared to the meager quantities available to the poor countries, it was foolish to conclude that America was a model which could be emulated, and absurd to believe that U.S.-style industrialization was a feasible goal for all nations.

Perhaps most important, we ignored the crucial fact that, while the U.S. was an oil-rich country, nearly all of the developing countries were oil-poor. During the 1950s, as the U.S. was powering its vast array of machines by consuming nearly half of the world's crude oil, only tiny trickles of oil were available to the poorer countries.

The wrongheadedness of the Superior Model Fallacy is revealed by a bottom-line analysis which was never made in the halcyon days of U.S. foreign aid when it was widely assumed there would be adequate resources in the future. Even a superficial evaluation would have demonstrated that this was a preposterous assumption: if the hoped-for miracle had occurred and every country were in a position to consume petroleum and minerals at the rate the U.S. was using them, all of the known reserves of these resources on earth would have been exhausted in less than a decade.

Yet this crucial calculation was never made, and the development effort muddled ahead under the pretense that if everything went well, all the world would someday enjoy a standard of living comparable to ours.

In retrospect, then, it is clear our plans for world development were based on monumental mistakes: we overlooked the importance of profound differences in cultural backgrounds; we ignored the crucial significance of vast disparities in available resources; we thought we had powers to influence the future of other countries that we in fact did not possess; we misjudged the influence of nature's bounty on our own history; and we were uncomprehending when poor countries which had limited resources and skimpy supplies of energy failed to march to our drums down the path of progress.

In 1973, William and Elizabeth Paddock, who de-

voted some of their prime years to the foreign aid
effort, wrote this terse epitaph for the Superior Model
Fallacy in their book *We Don't Know How:*

> Americans . . . forget the uniqueness of the American
> land. They forget that countries where we have gone
> to bring progress and development are what they are
> because of a lack of resources. The cultural stagnation
> there, which we are trying so hard to jog into life, is
> not the result of any inferiority in the caliber of its
> citizens. It is due to the harsh fact that those citizens
> have so little with which to build a modern nation.
> . . . They are trying to lift themselves up by their
> bootstraps when they have no boots.

The Paddocks have concluded that the fertility of
American land and the abundance of our mineral resources have instilled into Americans a supreme con-
fidence that we could remake the entire world in our
image. What has set America apart from nearly all
other nations is much more fundamental than spa-
cious skys and purple-mountained majesties. Our
uniqueness springs from soil so extraordinarily fe-
cund and mineral resources so great that the United
States became the world's largest producer of barium,
cadmium, coal, copper, feldspar, natural gas, gypsum,
lead, mica, molybdenum, petroleum, salt, silver, ti-
tanium, uranium, vanadium, phosphates and a vast
array of other ores. After three hundred years, the
myth of American superiority had become so pervasive that it took on a life of its own, independent of
the fabulous resources which had nurtured its development. As the Paddocks described the outcome of
the illusion,

> The resulting image of a country flowing with milk
> and honey made America the envy of the world. Im-
> migrants and native-born Americans alike came to
> believe that there really, truly, actually, honestly is a
> special quality that sets the American apart from
> everyone else on the globe, a quality often called
> Yankee ingenuity or get-up-and-go. . . . That quality,
> wedded to a superior technology, makes it possible, so
> goes the myth, for an American to do things no one
> else can do.

Actually, we might never have set ourselves up as a
superior model had U.S. planners placed our recent
history in proper perspective. Compared even with
the other advanced nations, the U.S. has been in a
class by itself. Energy consumption alone has made
us atypical in the postwar era. And we have been
recklessly using a grossly disproportionate share of
the world's petroleum at the same time that we have
been pursuing policies calculated to maximize the
consumption of energy in all phases of American life.

Our unique culture has been based on the assumption that the faster we found and used up our petroleum the better for everyone concerned. However,
even as we increased our overdependence on oil, we
relied increasingly on the rationalization that the nation's economic success was largely attributable to
American technical "know-how" and a special "mana-
gerial genius." This was a half truth which further
blurred our conception of ourselves. The whole truth
was that we were reaping the benefits of the prime
years of the Petroleum Age. Cheap, plentiful petroleum was the dynamo that made the great surge of
postwar prosperity possible. Cheap oil made every-

thing from air travel to petrochemicals to high-yield agriculture thrive, and huge new machines and processes that ran on oil were skimming the cream of the nation's high-grade raw materials as well.

Technological optimism was, nevertheless, so rampant in those days that it was thought that the long lead times required for development—which should have been measured in generations, not years—could somehow be drastically shortened. In other words, outlandish assumptions about technology and machines caused planners to assume the pace of development could be accelerated.

Had we understood our own history, we might have realized that the U.S. experience of the 1850s was far more relevant to the problems of most developing countries than the experience of the 1950s. We would have noted, for example, that the development of useful machines and the training of mechanics to maintain them must go hand in hand as part of a nation's orderly development. The early industrialization in the United States also reveals that gradualism is very important in any program of nation building: major steps in industrialization (the water-powered textile mill in the North is a good example) evolved step-wise out of the success of our agrarian frontier economy. In fact, our entire history teaches us that there can be no "great leap" into modernization, but this was overlooked by individuals whose attention was so captivated by the possibility of rapid change through new technological advances that they lost sight of the importance of energy and the necessity of one-step-at-a-time progress.

The Fat Man Fallacy

The final major misconception—we might accurately describe it as the Fat Man Fallacy—is a proposition nurtured by the advanced countries, especially the U.S., that the faster the rich countries consume the globe's resources the sooner the fruits of the general prosperity will be available to the poor nations. This rationalization was probably invented by the world's first rich man in order to persuade his neighbors to judge him not by his opulent lifestyle but by the number of servants and retainers he employed. Such reasoning has many advantages to a nation or an individual: it transmutes gluttony into an altruistic activity; it makes profligate behavior appear virtuous; it deftly sweeps offensive accusations under the rug of benevolence—and it soothes the consciences of those engaged in what Thorstein Veblen called conspicuous consumption.

Rich nations have long used this argument to justify their excesses, and the U.S. has developed ever more sophisticated variants of it as our consumption has reached higher and higher levels. Although the facts have given the lie to the Fat Man Fallacy every step along the way—the economic gap between the have and have-not nations has widened every year since the end of World War II—even today apologists for the superaffluent countries still rely upon its logic. Their politicians use the upbeat slogan "A rising tide lifts all the boats" to justify spiraling growth, and their economists devise fresh trickledown theories to explain how fat-nation gorging promotes the common good.

Predictably, the Fat Man Fallacy has become part of the folklore of American business, and a new species of special soothsayers has appeared to promulgate and expound its virtues. The most widely known of these self-styled futurologists is Herman Kahn. Kahn is a very clever man who is at his best when he is reassuring growth-oriented businessmen (or nations like Japan) that their activities make them great benefactors of mankind. His approach is not very original: he prepares simple-minded growth forecasts that project past trends into the future, and he corroborates these studies by collecting and collating the speculative "guesses" of individuals he deems to be Delphic.

In recent years Kahn has replaced the "trickle-down" rationale with what might be called a "drag-up" theory of economic advancement. He believes that if the rich countries can only continue expanding the GWP (Gross World Product) for another few decades, they will become so superaffluent that their economies will, willy-nilly, "drag the poor countries" into the realm of materialistic prosperity. Naturally, this cozy hypothesis has enormous appeal: it casts a warm, moral glow on the captains of superconsumption; it lets selfishness masquerade under the cloak of generosity; and it reassures everyone that sweeping solutions are possible to the big global problems.

Kahn tries to keep the Fat Man Fallacy thriving even when he must ignore plain evidence that scarcities are already dominating the world marketplace, for he is a true believer in the power of technology to "create" a resource cornucopia. He is contemptuous of those who talk of scarcities, and he harbors a special scorn for conservationists who hold to the quaint belief that nonrenewable resources like oil and minerals are actually nonrenewable.

In any event, the converts to Kahn's "drag-up" religion should be having some second thoughts. With the globe in the grip of an energy crunch, talk of technology opening doors to new storehouses of "inexhaustible" resources has a hollow ring—and the poor countries are acquiring a skeptical attitude toward rich neighbors who are buying their resources dirt cheap and making enormous profits processing them into finished products.

Despite all the efforts of Kahn and his ilk, the Fat Man Fallacy is being highlighted by events. Even unsophisticated leaders are beginning to realize that in a world of shortages there will be precious little left to trickle up or down to anyone if the rich nations continue their excessive resource consumption. The events of 1973–74 taught some brutal economic lessons to the poor countries which cannot be soothed by hypothetical projections of the future. They realize that the rich countries can make adjustments and pay "the going rate" for oil. They know they cannot—and they fear the end of cheap oil will bankrupt their economies and destroy their hopes.

As this ugly impasse deepens, the crossfire of the have-not countries will center inevitably on the swollen U.S. economy. The skimming of our own high-grade resources is "our business," but our ever-growing dependence on the resources of other countries may readily become the first item of business on the agenda of the raw materials cartels now being formed by groups of desperate have-not countries. We are already importing over 50 percent of six of the thirteen raw materials (bauxite, manganese, nickel, tin, zinc and chromium) considered vital for our industrial growth—and unless our demands slacken we will be importing over 50 percent of our oil, iron, lead and tungsten by 1985.

The appetites behind these statistics can only aggravate relations with countries beset by famines and shortages. The generous image that the U.S. has enjoyed is fading fast. Our new image is that of the corpulent diner demanding a third dessert as a hungry world watches at the window. Obviously, any conduct on our part that even suggests such a portrayal is indefensible. The Fat Man Fallacy must be discarded for the piece of historical nonsense that it is. Industrial production in the wealthy nations has been doubling every ten years. If this trend were to continue for fifty years, raw material demands would double five times, and require a volume of resource extraction thirty times greater than the present demands of affluent countries.

Reorientation: The Final Steps

The best way for the United States to respond to an energy-short world is to reorient its attitudes toward resources. The first step is to admit that priorities have been misassigned and that tragic miscalculations have been made. Technical "miracles" have been oversold to the world. The effect of explosive population increases on resource supplies has been largely ignored by industrial and poor nations alike— and the United States, more than any other country, has hastened the onset of global resource shortages. Our position of world leadership will be forfeited unless our national goals are scaled down and our outlook toward our neighbors is changed.

There are at least three basic changes to be made in U.S. policies. First, "big technology" solutions to the world's problems must be rejected. Automobiles, jet planes and even "green revolutions" are not paving stones to progress for have-not countries. The miscalculations of the green revolution, with its high-yield "miracle" seeds, makes the point. It was another panacea that was oversold; as a result, many people were misled. It offered assurance that population control programs weren't really important; it made poor countries dependent on the crucial resources (like oil and fertilizers) which they lacked; and it devastated their weak economies by exposing them to shocking increases in the prices of these vital commodities.

The green revolution is a high-risk venture. The new "miracle strains" of wheat and rice are vulnerable to pests or plant diseases that could produce agricultural catastrophes similar to the "late blight" which caused the Irish potato famine in the nineteenth century. More important, the green revolution requires large additional expenditures of energy for irrigation and fertilizers; for example, the extra fertilizer needs of India alone are so enormous that if that country applied fertilizer as intensively as the Netherlands its requirements would compel an overnight increase in world output by 50 percent.

The second change involves a turn toward the development and sharing of simple technologies. As China has already demonstrated, in the initial stages of nation building simple machines like water pumps and durable bicycles are more important than atomic reactors. The development of inexpensive devices to exploit wind and solar power is far more important than the building of steel mills or prestige skyscrapers.

Finally, what is needed most in the 1970s is not new scientific cure-alls, but joint efforts in self-restraint. The United States must accept an energy diet and learn to go lean. No longer can this country (or any other industrialized nation) "eat up" resources desperately needed by an already overpopulated world. By contrast, the poor countries must contemplate a different kind of self-restraint and admit once and for all that their prospects are hopeless unless they mount emergency programs to control increases in their populations. The history of India in the last quarter century says it all. In the postwar period, the U.S. alone has spent about $10 billion on economic aid to India. Yet, largely due to inept efforts to curb population increases, the per capita income in India has hardly increased at all.

In the poor nations of the world, it is estimated that

malnutrition affects 60 percent of the population, with horrible human costs in mental and physical retardation. Unless population is checked very soon, there is virtually no hope that these governments will be able to feed their people. And even if one assumes that all of the U.S. agricultural surpluses will be given to these countries, it will be impossible to feed the swollen populations now foreseen. In such a situation, famine casts an ominous shadow over whole continents.

The have-not nations of the world are now in the grip of trends that are propelling them toward chaos and calamity. If these trends continue, there is a growing danger that reckless authoritarian governments—elitist or revolutionary regimes—will dominate their politics. This darkening prospect for the underdeveloped portions of the world holds more than moral and humanitarian implications for the advanced countries. Professor Robert L. Heilbroner has recently compared the present international economic–political situation to a large train in which a few travelers from the industrialized countries ride in extraordinary comfort in the plush first-class section while the masses of passengers are bunched in cattle cars. In *An Inquiry into the Human Prospect,* Heilbroner suggests this probable outcome:

> To the governments of revolutionary regimes, however, the passengers in the first-class coaches not only ride at their ease but have decorated their compartments and enrich their lives by using the work and appropriating the resources of the masses who ride be-

hind them. Such governments are not likely to view
the vast differences between first class and cattle class
with the forgiving eyes of their predecessors; and
whereas their sense of historical injustice might be of
little account in a world in which economic impotence also meant military impotence, it takes on entirely new dimensions in the coming decades for reasons connected with the changing technology of war.

The new factor which now must be taken into account in this tragic equation is the capability of vola-
tile poor nations to obtain nuclear materials and
fashion crude nuclear weapons. So armed, countries
with limited prospects and little to risk would be
tempted to break into the first-class compartment and
use nuclear blackmail to extract concessions and force
a redistribution of wealth. Whether such nuclear
blackmail is practiced by revolutionary governments,
there is the increasing prospect that terrorist organizations will attempt to obtain such materials and
build nucelar weapons to further their own desperate
ends.

When Professor Heilbroner's analysis appeared in
January 1974, he stated that "there seems little doubt
that some nuclear capability will be in the hands of
the major underdeveloped nations, certainly within
the next few decades and perhaps much sooner." The
example of China was cited as a nation joining the
nuclear family uninvited. This timetable is already
being hastily revised. On May 18, 1974, India became
the sixth country in the world to detonate a nuclear
bomb. Before the shockwaves of this explosion had
even ceased, other events virtually assured the accel-

erated proliferation of nuclear capacity among the underdeveloped nations. President Nixon, dispensing favors like some summertime Santa Claus, promised Egypt a nuclear plant, and later during his 1974 Middle East tour made a similar offer of technological largesse to Israel. Then the nervous ruler of oil-rich Iran announced an agreement with France to purchase nuclear power plants and indicated that nuclear weapons development would follow.

As the Indian explosion demonstrated, the road to nuclear weapons is wide open to the country that has a conventional nuclear reactor, even a small, so-called "research" facility such as Canada built for India in the 1950s. The key factor in moving from the peaceful generation of electricity in nuclear reactors to atomic weapons and terrorist materials is plutonium. Plutonium is an invariable by-product of every uranium-powered reactor and is produced when the fissioning isotope of uranium releases a neutron which is absorbed by natural uranium. With plutonium in hand, the construction of a bomb is not a difficult task for knowledgeable physicists.

While plutonium is not automatically available from the neighborhood reactor, it is not necessary to build an expensive facility like a uranium enrichment plant to get weapons-grade nuclear materials. Following the Indian lead, bomb materials can be quietly diverted from the irradiated wastes of an ordinary atomic power reactor. Today there is plutonium being produced continually in the nuclear power plants that operate in fifteen countries throughout the world. This number of atomic-powered nations is expected to nearly triple according to present plans, reinforcing the likelihood of additional governments diverting materials to develop a nuclear weapons capability. More countries with atomic power plants and more reactors in each nation vastly increases the volume of irradiated wastes which will be transported for necessary reprocessing.

Such proliferation makes outright theft or hijacking of even greater concern than governmental diversion. With increasing amounts of plutonium moving about the world, terrorists and criminals—as well as governments themselves—are given the opportunity to steal these illicit materials. Plutonium, of course, need not be turned into a bomb in order to be used as a weapon of extortion and blackmail, as it is extremely poisonous in powdered form. While the threat of punitive retaliation may act as a deterrent in the case of governments in underdeveloped countries, such constraints are worthless in controlling a zealous terrorist.

In the U.S., the nuclear future of mankind is increasingly being viewed as more of a Pandora's box than a new Promethean promise. Internationally, it is the height of folly to pursue a foreign policy that exports fission before fertilizer, and promotes the sale of exotic and expensive hardware when the need is for practical goods and ideas to sustain life. More ironic would be the irresponsible proliferation of nuclear swords forged from our own atomic materials exported as plowshares.

The problems before the human family have already reached staggering proportions. With a world population of approximately 3.7 billion that at current rates is doubling in one generation, there is no hope of achieving world stability unless the population spiral is quickly slackened. The whole human enterprise is a machine without brakes, for there are no indications that the world's political leaders will deal with the realities until catastrophes occur. The rich countries are using resources with an extravagant disregard for the next generation; and the poor countries appear to be incapable of acting to curb the population increases that are erasing their hope for a better future. In such a world, declarations and manifestos which ignore the imperatives of the limits of growth are empty exercises. All the available evidence says we have already passed a point of no return, and tragic human convulsions are at hand.

The present American model must be drastically revised. As a model for the underdeveloped nations, an industrial-based, energy-intensive American agricultural system that is dependent upon fuel-gobbling machines and petrochemical fertilizers must be replaced with a practical plan which utilizes simpler tools and technology, and harnesses the natural flow of energy in more productive ways. In an industrialized food system, from twenty-five to five hundred times more energy must be used to produce one unit of energy in the form of food than in primitive cultures. If all nations copied our agricultural example, nearly four-fifths of present world energy supplies would have to be devoted to food production.

The United States is confronted with a large challenge: we must realize that we cannot continue to consume the commodities of the world at superaffluent levels. The challenge is not only one of charitable concern, but of protective self-interest as well. Without the restraint of curbed consumption as well as controlled world population growth, international instability will mount, authoritarian regimes will proliferate, and sporadic political terrorism will be inevitable.

A stable, hopeful world is impossible unless the illusions that have prevented concerted action are cast aside. The energy crisis is a lightning bolt which has illuminated this truth. Today the resources to feed the present population of this planet are lacking. Today there is not enough petroleum—or other available energy sources—to make industrialization a rational goal for the have-not nations in the foreseeable future.

chapter ten

NOTES ON A NATIONAL ENERGY POLICY

"To these virtues we shall return in the ordeal through which we must now pass, or all that still remains will be lost and all that we attempt, in order to defend it, will be in vain. We shall turn from the soft vices in which a civilization decays, we shall return to the stern virtues by which a civilization is made, we shall do this because, at long last, we know that we must, because finally we begin to see that the hard way is the only enduring way."

—Walter Lippmann
1940

If our assessment is even half right, a fundamental reorientation is necessary in the next few years. But how should changes be initiated? This is the crucial question as the debate over a national energy policy intensifies.

As we have seen, major changes will be required in every sector of American life. The energy crisis is too profound and pervasive for patchwork remedies or piecemeal solutions. With the cooperation of the states, the President and the Congress must pass the laws and enunciate the priorities needed to bring a workable national energy policy into being.

As we should have learned in the winter of 1974, the hour is already late. The sooner basic reforms are instituted the better. Energy "lead times" are unusually long—most of the decisions of the 1970s have already been made—so serious disruptions are being risked each week action is delayed. Permanent gasoline rationing, for example, will probably be necessary unless the trend toward small cars is greatly accelerated in the next three or four years.

The national policy we need must be all-inclusive, and it must cut through all the misleading arguments advanced by spokesmen for the energy industries about alternate "growth track" scenarios and the "environmental trade-offs." Such arguments have only one aim: to garner public and governmental support for future expansion projects. A viable energy program must explicitly repeal and reject the old policies, which have made our energy system the most wasteful in the world. It must be simple and sweeping and encompass everything from land use to architecture to the size of motor vehicles. It will be a marching order for America, and it can be stated in twenty-six words:

> It is the policy of the United States to use energy re-
> sources with the highest degree of efficiency, and to
> conserve energy whenever and wherever possible.

Of course, such a declaration will be meaningless unless it is accompanied by a wholesale revamping of the obsolete pricing policies, subsidies, and tax laws which substantially determine the production and use of energy in this country. The existing the-more-you-use-the-less-you-pay pricing policies have encouraged energy squandering by big users of natural gas and electricity. More than 50 percent of the sales of natural gas, for example, are made under "sweetheart" discounts to industrial users. An end to this practice would lower prices for other consumers, would free more natural gas for use by homeowners, and would provide a strong incentive for industrial thrift. Across the board reforms in pricing policies for gas and electricity would be one of the most effective—and least disruptive—means of promoting the large-scale conservation of our energy supplies.

Similarly, the repeal of the many tax statutes, subsidy arrangements, and regulations which encourage the inefficient use of energy and favor the most profligate segments of U.S. industry would give a powerful impetus to conservation. Energy efficiency must take precedence. The big tax breaks and subsidies should go to those industries, technologies, and national programs which are helping the country eliminate waste and become more economical in its use of energy. For example, homeowners who install solar energy facilities (and not oilmen who deplete oil) should be favored by our tax code, and the big transportation subsidies should go to mass transit, not highways.

Once the U.S. begins to implement such a new national policy, it will set the stage for the change we have outlined in this book. It will end urban sprawl and reorient concepts about the design and function of cities; it will enforce basic reforms in the methods and purposes of industrial production; and it will release this nation from a dangerous overreliance on the resources of other countries. So, too, it will quicken the recycling of all industrial and household wastes; will encourage the transition to the manufacture of long-lasting consumer goods; and will also hasten the development of highly efficient new machines and industrial processes.

The proper energy policy will inculcate energy-saving plans and practices in all aspects of American life. It will also redirect the aims of the energy industries. The natural gas industry, for example, will take pride—and profit—in prolonging the availability of gas supplies for U.S. homeowners (overwhelmingly the highest and best use for this fossil fuel). The electric power companies will stop measuring their success by increases in their "growth loads" and gain satisfaction and economic reward by keeping electric rates reasonable and operating the most efficient electric systems in the world. And once the oil industry is weaned away from its mindless policy of depleting our vital petroleum resources as fast as possible, it, too, might win praise for its conservation achievements if it extends the "life span" of the remaining petroleum resources twice as far as contemplated by the experts.

A forward-looking national energy policy will reinvigorate American life. It will also provide the framework for a leaner, more mature society. Many neglected values—and many creative opportunities for human initiative—will come to the forefront as national aims and goals are transformed. As the country turns away from its fixation on maximizing production and keying personal fulfillments to consumerism, an exciting series of new challenges will confront all citizens. Our national attitudes toward the environment and the management of resources will be drastically altered as the country realizes the bankruptcy of the proposed policy of keeping the big energy spree going by ransacking the continental shelves of petroleum reserves that should be saved for our children.

The end of the era of cheap energy is already producing worldwide changes in the patterns of industrial growth. In the next decade, much of the world's additional manufacturing of such basic products as petrochemicals, aluminum, steel, fertilizers, and other big energy-using processes will shift to the oil-rich countries. This diversification will force the U.S. to concentrate its inventiveness on a service-oriented economy which specializes in energy-thrifty, advanced technologies and knowledge-intensive industries.

Such a reorientation will do more than change modes of production—it has the potential to alter the national agenda as well. The decline of the Petroleum Age should compel this country, at last, to turn to the central task of building handsome, balanced, life-giving cities. This is a crowning achievement of any great culture, and hopefully the rethinking and reshaping of our cities will become a principal endeavor of American life in the years ahead. This adventure could involve everyone in the kind of action and planning which could make individual lives richer as people work together to enlarge what the ancient Greeks referred to as "the public happiness."

As has been the case throughout human history, shortages and scarcities challenge the members of a society to act together in creative ways. As the changes get underway, however, Americans will realize how flawed and anti-human our old system of undisciplined growth was. It had no brakes. It made increases in production and the expansion of Gross National Product into a secular god which was worshipped at the altar of its own affluence. It treated consumption and mobility as the be-alls and end-alls of human life. And it de-emphasized the common purposes and ethical values which are the cement of any community.

Is this agenda achievable? The skeptics say it is not. Some argue that energy belt-tightening is a prescription for mass unemployment; others assert reliance on less energy means asking the American people to give up their standard of living; and still others are convinced the U.S. political system is so attuned to the wants and aims of rising affluence it cannot respond adequately to a nagging energy crisis. Put bluntly, this argument reads: "No politician can vote for proposals that require people to give up their goodies and be re-elected!" These are crucial, interrelated questions, and they deserve careful evaluation.

The nation's largest electric utility stated the argument of old-guard industrialists in a full-page ad in major U.S. newspapers in the spring of 1974. It read:

> There is no more nonsensical a concept than "generate less energy" as a solution to our energy crisis. . . . Just start listening to the critics of our society, start generating less energy, and the plummet begins. Less production, fewer jobs, lower demand for products, followed by still further diminished production and galloping unemployment until America is eventually reduced to the hard life.

This scare argument will be repeated again and again in the months ahead. However, it is based on fear and it ignores the real issues. As was found in the winter of 1974, growth which ignores limits is the real threat to steady employment in a time of intractable energy shortages. The real victims of the Arab embargo were the tens of thousands of auto and airline employees who were suddenly thrown out of work. A well-planned national program of orderly conservation will mean gradual shifts and a different job mix in industry. The building of fewer cars and trucks and more buses and trains need not mean unemployment if it is part of a well-conceived transportation transition, just as thousands of new jobs in recycling industries can offset declines in employment in companies producing virgin raw materials.

The worst mistake that could be made would be to

cling to the status quo. A conservation-oriented economy will provide a wider range of jobs that are more fulfilling to individual workers. An employment increase in service industries and a greater demand for highly skilled craftsmen should be good news. It will mean a shorter work week, working environments that are less dehumanizing, and a dramatic increase in opportunities for individual creativity.

The changes implicit in a national energy policy of conservation need not undermine the vital elements of our standard of living. Belt-tightening is invariably a useful exercise for an individual or a society which is extravagant. Basic household conveniences, for example, need not be sacrificed if big energy savings are made by ending unnecessary travel and producing goods that are more durable. A slower-paced, more frugal America that puts less store in excessive mobility or in the ownership of junky goods and spends more of its energies on work that makes its immediate social and physical environment better will be an America that is more at peace with itself and with the world.

Up to this point most U.S. politicians have elected to use the big oil companies as a scapegoat. This has enabled them to duck the tough issues surrounding a national energy policy of self-denial. In a democracy it is extremely difficult to tackle a critical national problem if the President denies its existence and the Congress avoids facing the responsibility of being the bearer of "bad news" and the leader in the quest for a more frugal lifestyle. Thus, Richard

Nixon let Congress off the hook by insisting that the energy crisis is a "one-time, short-term problem."

These failures have postponed the big debate. The real test of the political system will come in three or four years when the full magnitude of the problem manifests itself here and abroad. It is our belief that events will force the next Presidents to acknowledge the imperatives of conservation and propose a vigorous national energy policy for the nation. Once shortages—and the economic consequences of shortages—certify the scope of the crisis, political action will be galvanized. Everyone will then realize that the country is running out of oil and that neither presidential sloganeering nor the castigating of the oil companies can increase the output of petroleum. This development will serve notice on public officials that the politics of "more" must give way to a new politics of national thrift.

Once again a significant segment of the people is ahead of the politicians. A new mood already is changing the attitudes of Americans. Their efforts to redefine the good life are exhibited in the no-growth, slow-growth movement, which views further sprawl or increases in population as a prime threat to the environment, and in the anti-materialistic attitudes of a younger generation which is "turned off" by the self-indulgence of its elders. These citizens, and others who esteem quality living over empty consumerism, are ready now to support the changes a national energy policy will entail.

This movement is a growing force in American

life. Calling for deliberate decision making and reforms that will change U.S. lifestyles, it explicitly
rejects the supertechnologist's idea that "If we can
do it, it must be done." It led the fight against the
SST and considers that victory both a demonstration
of energy foresight and ecological common sense. It
is also determined that the resources owned by all
of the people (and the bulk of our unexploited fossil
fuels now lie beneath publicly owned lands) will be
developed both with restraint and with an eye to
the needs of future generations.

A conservative, deliberate approach is imperative.
Many conventional energy decisions made today will
affect us for fifty years; and nuclear plants already
built have created what can only be described as
"thousand-year" problems. Clearly, the U.S. has never
had a national energy policy, and it is an act of
consummate irresponsibility to continue making long-
range decisions without sober guidelines to direct
our choices.

We will commit a tragic error if we plunge ahead
with current plans for nuclear expansion without
examining the solar-wind option as a substitute. The
sun is a free, renewable, zero-environmental-impact
alternative. Experts have calculated that, if we could
convert all the solar energy that reaches the earth
every twenty-four hours to electricity or other usable
forms of energy, it would be worth roughly half a
trillion dollars each day measured by current prices.
The number one energy scandal of the 1970s is the
effort of the nuclear power advocates to belittle the

vast potential of solar energy. There is a growing body of evidence that, if we were spending the money now being expended on breeder reactor research and development on solar and wind technologies, remarkable results could be achieved in ten or fifteen years.

If this alternative is viable, it offers an infinitely safer and saner path for humankind.

On the other hand, the perils of nuclear proliferation loom larger each month. This country is aggressively selling nuclear plants to unstable countries which lack the engineering expertise to operate them according to U.S. safety standards. Yet, the scientific brinkmen who are pushing nuclear proliferation pretend the only real policy issue concerns the likelihood of remote engineering accidents. The real issues—fateful issues that can put the whole human enterprise in permanent peril—are infinitely larger and more frightening. In addition, new studies of the possibilities of nuclear terrorism suggest that the so-called "peaceful uses" of nuclear energy are far more risky and unreliable than the fearful weapons controlled by the few nations belonging to the "atomic club." Conditions in today's unstable world are creating new terrorist groups—and could ultimately spawn terrorist nations—which could readily gain access to bomb-grade materials and turn to nuclear blackmail as a political weapon.

An equally awesome problem concerns the handling and disposal of the huge mass of lethal radioactive wastes which are produced by nuclear installations around the globe. These materials, some of which will last for tens of thousands of years, will place an impossible burden on the frail human institutions which will be their unwitting custodians. What gives this generation the right to enjoy energy now and bequeath to millennia of unborn inhabitants the terrifying task of handling our "wastes"? This issue should not be decided by arrogant engineers. It is a paramount problem for philosophers and statesmen—and, indeed, for all of us.

The case for a lean America is also the case for a go-slow, conservation-oriented approach to the whole energy problem. The time has come to call a halt to decision making by discredited technological super-optimists. Over a century ago, the great French physiologist, Claude Bernard, advised his fellow scientists, "True science teaches us to doubt, and in ignorance to refrain."

This axiom contains a message we must take to heart if there is to be a rational future.

NOTES FOR READERS

As we acknowledged in the beginning, this is a consciously provocative book. We have taken a polemical stance because we are convinced that decisive action will be taken only if the right arguments are boldly advanced. If we have succeeded in this effort, many readers may want to examine more closely the complex and controversial issues of the energy crisis.

What follows is a partial list of energy or energy-related books. It is not a definitive list, but it does contain many of the most readily available works.

A more extensive bibliography, one that attempted to measure the total cultural and ecological relationship, would lead readers to the obvious classics by Lewis Mumford and Jane Jacobs and to more recent works by Daniel J. Boorstin and Robert L. Heilbroner. But since energy is such a new subject and so few nontechnical books have been written for the student or reader seeking a more general, broader approach, we are focusing our list on books and publications that discuss the energy problem with an emphasis on history, consumption and future possibilities and limitations.

General Books

The subject is permeated by so many statistics and dense technical topics that until recently few good books for the general reader were written. Two books published in 1974 have the scope and detail to provide an overview. They are David Freeman's *Energy: The New Era* and Wilson Clark's *Energy for Survival*. Another recent work which explores the scientific and technological basis of the energy dilemma is *Energy and the Future* by Hammond, Metz and Maugh.

Two probing books which wrestle with the philosophical and political problems of the human predicament produced by the population-food-resources-pollution crunch are Robert L. Heilbroner's *An Inquiry into the Human Prospect* and *Ecology and the Politics of Scarcity*, by William Ophuls, which will appear in 1975. These studies complement the two best ecology books of the 1970s, *Population, Resources and Environment* by Paul and Ann Ehrlich, and *The Closing Circle* by Barry Commoner.

Finally, three very different studies which put crucial future problems in perspective are the controversial *The Limits to Growth* by Meadows, Randers and Jorgen (a study of the carrying capacity of planet earth sponsored by the Club of Rome); an analysis of the impact of U.S. demographic trends, *Population and the American Future*, the farsighted report of the first U.S. Commission to study our population problems and policies; and *We Don't Know How*, a critique of U.S. foreign assistance programs by William and Elizabeth Paddock.

A highly original work, which elucidates the "net energy" concept and its consequences, is Howard T. Odum's *Environment, Power and Society*, and a statistical compilation which dramatizes the dangers of exponential growth is Ralph Lapp's *The Logarithmic Century*.

Specialized Studies

Until recently the skirmish over the future nuclear power was largely confined to periodicals. Two very recent books which explore the awesome dangers of atomic terrorism are *The Curve of Binding Energy* by John McPhee, and *Nuclear Theft, Risks and Safeguards* by Theodore B. Taylor, a recent defector from the closed world of the nuclear establishment.

Excellent articles on solar energy are beginning to appear, but the only major work on this vital topic was written a decade ago by the late Farrington Daniels. It bears the title *Direct Use of the Sun's Energy*.

Transportation is another neglected area. A good recent work, which makes the case for a rail renaissance, is *The Way We Go: The Coming Revival of U.S. Rail Passenger Service* by Southerland and McCleery.

In the nonbook field, many of the recently released

studies and reports of the Energy Policy Project of
the Ford Foundation, and the April 1974 issue of
Science Magazine, contain useful analyses of many
aspects of the energy crisis.

DATE DUE

MAR 3 0 '84